Reach Your Potential
CANCER

Teresa Moorey

Dedication

For my eldest son, Daniel,

for my friend Sylvia

and for Molly Moorey, my mother-in-law

Also, in memory of Diana, Princess of Wales, who exemplified many caring Cancerian traits

ISBN 0 340 69712 1

First published 1998
Impression number 10 9 8 7 6 5 4 3 2 1
Year   2001   2000   1999 1998

Typeset by Transet Limited, Coventry, England.
Printed in Great Britain for Hodder & Stoughton Educational, a division of Hodder Headline plc, 338 Euston Road, London NW1 3BH by Cox and Wyman, Reading, Berks.

Contents

Introduction

A PERSPECTIVE OF ASTROLOGY

Interest in the mystery and significance of the heavens is perhaps as old as humanity. If we can cast our imaginations back, to a time when there were no street lamps, televisions or even books, if we can picture how it must have been to have nothing to do through the deep nights of winter other than to sit and weave stories by the fire at the cave mouth, then we can come close to sensing how important the great dome of stars must have seemed in ancient times.

We are prone to believe that we are wiser today, having progressed beyond old superstitions. We know that all stars are like our Sun – giant nuclear reactors. We know that the planets are lumps of rock reflecting sunlight, they are not gods or demons. But how wise are we in truth? Our growing accumulation of facts brings us no closer to discovering the real meaning behind life. It may well be that our cave-dwelling ancestors knew better than us the meaning of holism. The study of astrology may be part of a journey towards a more holistic perception, taking us, as it does, through the fertile, and often uncharted realms of our own personality.

Until the seventeenth century astrology (which searches for the meaning of heavenly patterns) and astronomy (which seeks to clarify facts about the skies) were one, and it was the search for meanings, not facts that inspired the earliest investigations. Lunar phases have been found carved on bone and stone figures from as early as 15,000BCE (Before Common Era). Astrology then evolved through the civilisations of Mesopotamia and Greece among others.

Through the 'dark ages' much astrological lore was preserved in Islamic countries, but in the fifteenth century astrology grew in popularity in the West. Queen Elizabeth I had her own personal astrologer, John Dee, and such fathers of modern astronomy as Kepler and Galileo served as court astrologers in Europe.

Astrology was taught at the University of Salamanca until 1776. What is rarely appreciated is that some of our greatest scientists, notably Newton and even Einstein, were led to their discoveries by intuition. Newton was a true mystic, and it was the search for meaning – the same motivation that inspired the Palaeolithic observer – that gave rise to some of our most brilliant advances. Indeed Newton is widely believed to have been an astrologer. The astronomer Halley, who discovered the famous comet, is reported to have criticised Newton for this, whereupon Sir Isaac replied 'I have studied it Sir, you have not!'

During the twentieth century astrology enjoyed a revival, and in 1948 The Faculty of Astrological Studies was founded, offering tuition of high quality and an examination system. The great psychologist Carl Jung was a supporter of astrology, and his work has expanded ideas about the mythic connections of the birth chart. Astrology is still eyed askance by many people, and there is no doubt that there is little purely scientific corroboration for astrology – the exception to this is the exhaustive statistical work undertaken by the Gauquelins. Michel Gauquelin was a French statistician whose research shows undeniable connection between professional prominence and the position of planets at birth. Now that the concept of a mechanical universe is being superseded, there is a greater chance that astrology and astronomy will reunite.

Anyone who consults a good astrologer comes away deeply impressed by the insight of the birth chart. Often it is possible to see very deeply into the personality and to be able to throw light on current dilemmas. It is noteworthy that even the most sceptical of people tend to know their Sun sign and the characteristics associated with it.

■ WHAT IS A BIRTH CHART?

Your birth chart is a map of the heavens drawn up for the time, date and place of your birth. An astrologer will prefer you to be as accurate as you can about the time of day, for that affects the sign rising on the eastern horizon. This 'rising sign' is very important to your personality. However, if you do not know your birth time a chart can still be compiled for you. There will be some details missing, but useful interpretations may still be made. It is far better for the astrologer to know that your birth time is in question than to operate from a position of false certainty. The birth chart for Diana, Princess of Wales (page 4) is a simplified chart. Additional factors would be entered on the chart and considered by an astrologer, such as angles (aspects) between the planets, and the houses.

The birth chart shows each of the planets and the Moon in the astrological signs, and can be thought of as an 'energy map' of the different forces operating within the psyche. Thus the Sun sign (often called 'birth sign' or 'star sign') refers only to the position of the Sun. If the planets are in very different signs from the Sun sign, the interpretation will be greatly modified. Thus, if a person has Sun in Leo yet is somewhat introverted or quiet, this may be because the Moon was in reserved Capricorn when that person was born. Nonetheless, the Sun represents the light of consciousness, the integrating force, and most people recognise that they are typical of their Sun sign, although in some people it will be more noticeable than in others. The planets Mercury and Venus are very

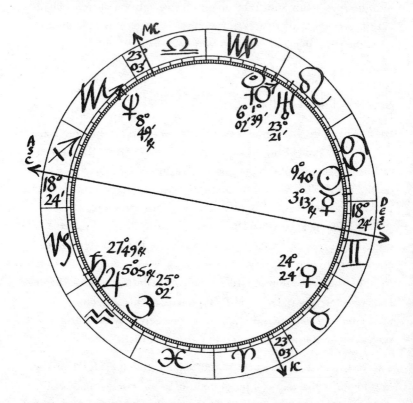

The chart of Diana, Princess of Wales
The Princess had Sun and Mercury in Cancer. However, Sagittarius rising
gave her a sense of adventure and an interest in keeping fit.

close to the Sun and often occupy the same sign, so intensifying the
Sun sign influence, if this is the case.

This book is written about your Sun sign, because the Sun sign
serves as an accessible starting point for those wishing to learn
about themselves through astrology. However, do not let your interest
stop there. If you find anything helpful in comments and advice
stemming from Sun sign alone, you will find your true birth chart

The **planets** are life principles, energy centres. To enable you to understand the birth chart, here are their glyphs:

Sun	☉	Jupiter	♃
Moon	☽	Saturn	♄
Mercury	☿	Uranus	♅
Venus	♀	Neptune	♆
Mars	♂	Pluto	♇ (Ǝ)

Rising Sign or **Ascendant** (**ASC**) is the way we have of meeting the world, our outward persona. **Midheaven** (**MC**) refers to our image, aspirations, how we like to be seen.

The **signs** are modes of expression, ways of being. Here are their glyphs:

Aries	♈	Libra	♎
Taurus	♉	Scorpio	♏
Gemini	♊	Sagittarius	♐
Cancer	♋	Capricorn	♑
Leo	♌	Aquarius	♒
Virgo	♍	Pisces	♓

Using knowledge of the glyphs you can see that the Sun is in Cancer in our example birth chart (page 4).

even more revealing. The address of the Faculty of Astrological Studies appears in 'Further Reading' at the back of this book, and it is a good idea to approach them for a list of trained astrologers who can help you. Moon *phase* at birth (as distinct from Moon sign) is also very important. *The Moon and You for Beginners* (see 'Further Reading') explains this fascinating area clearly, and provides a simple chart for you to look up your Moon phase, and learn what this means for your personality.

■ HOW DOES ASTROLOGY WORK?

We cannot explain astrology by the usual methods of cause and effect. In fact, there are many things we cannot explain. No one can define exactly what life is. We do not know exactly what electricity is, but we know how to use it. Few of us have any idea how a television set works, but we know how to turn it on. Although we are not able to explain astrology we are still able to use it, as any capable astrologer will demonstrate.

Jung discovered something called 'synchronicity'. This he defined as 'an acausal connecting principle'. Simply, this means that some events have a meaningful connection *other than cause and effect*. The planets do not cause us to do things, but their movements are synchronistic with our lives. The old dictum 'as above, so below' applies here. It is a mystery. We can't explain it, but that doesn't mean we should refuse to believe in it. A little boy on a visit to the circus saw an elephant for the first time and said 'There's no such thing'. We may laugh at the little boy, but how many of us respond to things we do not understand in this way?

The planetary positions in your birth chart are synchronistic with the time of your birth, when you took on separate existence, and they are synchronistic with your individuality in this life. They have much to say about you.

■ MYTH AND PSYCHOLOGY

The planets are named after the old gods and goddesses of Rome, which in turn link in with Greek and other pantheons. The planets represent 'life principles' – forces that drive the personality, and as such they can be termed 'archetypal'. This means that they are basic ideas, universal within human society and are also relevant in terms of the forces that, in some inexplicable way, inhabit the corners of the universe and inform the Earth and all human institutions. Thus the assertive energy that is represented by Mars means energetic action of all sorts – explosions and fires, wars, fierce debates and personal anger. Put briefly, here are the meanings of the planets:

- Mercury – intellect and communication
- Venus – love, unifying, relating
- Mars – assertion, energy, fighting spirit
- Jupiter – expansion, confidence, optimism
- Saturn – limitation, discipline
- Uranus – rebellion, independence
- Neptune – power to seek the ideal, sense the unseen
- Pluto – power to transform and evolve

These principles are modified according to the astrological sign they inhabit; thus Venus in Pisces may be gently loving, dreamy and self-sacrificing, while Venus in Aries will be demanding and adventurous in relationships. Thus the planets in signs form a complex psychological framework – and that is only part of the story of chart interpretation!

In the old mythologies these 'energies' or 'archetypes' or 'gods' were involved in classical dramas. An example is the story of Saturn and Uranus. Uranus is the rejecting father of Saturn, who later castrates and murders his father – thus innovative people reject reactionaries, who then murder them, so the revolutionary part of the personality is continually 'killed off' by the restrictive part. The exact positions and angles between the planets will indicate how this and other myths may come to life. In addition, the mere placement of planets by sign – and, of course, especially the Sun sign, call forth various myths as illustrations. The ancient myths are good yarns, but they are also inspired and vivid dramatisations of what may be going on repeatedly within your personality and that of your nearest and dearest. Myths are used by many modern psychologists and thera-pists in a tradition that has grown since Jung. We shall be using mythic themes to illustrate internal dynamics in this book.

■ THE SIGNS OF THE ZODIAC

There are twelve signs, and each of these belongs to an Element –
Earth, Fire, Air or Water, and a Quality – Cardinal, Fixed or
Mutable. The Cardinal signs are more geared to action, the Fixed
tend to remain stable and rooted, whereas the Mutable signs are
adaptable, changeable.

SIGN	QUALITY	ELEMENT
Aries	Cardinal	Fire
Taurus	Fixed	Earth
Gemini	Mutable	Air
Cancer	Cardinal	Water
Leo	Fixed	Fire
Virgo	Mutable	Earth
Libra	Cardinal	Air
Scorpio	Fixed	Water
Sagittarius	Mutable	Fire
Capricorn	Cardinal	Earth
Aquarius	Fixed	Air
Pisces	Mutable	Water

Jung defined four functions of consciousness – four different ways
of perceiving the world – 'thinking', 'feeling', 'sensation' and
'intuition'. Thinking is the logical, evaluative approach that works
in terms of the mind. Feeling is also evaluative, but this time in
relation to culture and family needs. This is not the same as emotion,
although 'feeling' people often process emotions more smoothly
than other types. Jung saw 'feeling' as rational, too. 'Sensation'
refers to the 'here and now', the five physical senses, while
'intuition' relates to the possible, to visions and hunches. Jung
taught that we tend to have one function uppermost in conscious-

ness, another one or maybe two secondary and another repressed or 'inferior', although we all possess each of these functions to some degree.

Jungian ideas are being refined and expanded, and they are incorporated into modern methods of personality testing, as in the Myers-Briggs test. If a prospective employer has recently given you such a test, it was to establish your talents and potential for the job. However, the basic four-fold division is still extremely useful, and I find it is often of great help in assisting clients to understand themselves, and their partners, in greater depth – for we are all apt to assume that everyone processes information and applies it in the same way as we do. But they don't! It is worthy of mention that the important categories of 'introverted' and 'extraverted' were also identified by Jung. In astrology, Fire and Air signs seem to be extraverted, generally speaking, and Earth and Water introverted – and this has been borne out by the statistical research of the astrologer, Jeff Mayo. However, this doesn't mean that all feeling and sensation people are introverted and all intuitives and thinkers extraverted – this is definitely not the case, and calls for more detailed examination of the chart (e.g. lots of Fire and Water may mean an extravert feeling type).

Very broadly speaking we may link the Fire signs to intuition, Water to feeling, Earth to sensation and Air to thinking. Often thinking and feeling are drawn together and sensation and intuition are attracted, because they are opposites. This probably happens because we all seek to become more whole, but the process can be painful. The notion of the four functions, when understood, does help to throw light on some of the stumbling blocks we often encounter in relationships. However, some people just do not seem to fit. Also Fire doesn't always correspond to intuition, Water to feeling, etc. – it seems this is usually the case, but not all astrologers agree. Some link Fire with feeling, Water with intuition, and most agree that other chart factors are also important. As with all theories, this can be used to help, expand and clarify, not as a rigid system to impose definitions. We shall be learning more about these matters in relation to the Sun sign in the following pages.

■ THE PRECESSION OF THE EQUINOXES

One criticism often levelled at astrology is that 'the stars have moved' and so the old signs are invalid. There is some truth in this, and it is due to a phenomenon called 'The Precession of the Equinoxes'. The beginning of the sign Aries occurs when the Sun is overhead at the equator, moving northwards. This is called the Spring Equinox, for now day and night are equal all over the globe, and the first point of Aries is called the 'equinoctial point'. Because the Earth not only turns on its axis but 'rocks' on it (imagine a giant knitting needle driven through the poles – the Earth spins on this, but the head of the needle also slowly describes a circle in space) the 'equinoctial point' has moved against the background of stars. Thus, when the Sun is overhead at the equator, entering Aries, it is no longer at the start of the constellation of Aries, where it occurred when the signs were named, but is now in the constellation of Pisces. The 'equinoctial point' is moving backwards into Aquarius, hence the idea of the dawning 'Aquarian age'.

So where does that leave astrology? Exactly in the same place, in actuality. For it all depends on how you think the constellations came to be named in the first place. Did our ancestors simply look up and see the shape of a Ram in the sky? Or did they – being much more intuitive and in tune with their surroundings than we are – feel sharply aware of the quality, the energies around at a certain time of the year, and *then* look skyward, translating what they sensed into a suitable starry symbol? This seems much more likely – and you have only to look at the star groups to see that it takes a fair bit of imagination to equate most of them with the figures they represent! The Precession of the Equinoxes does not affect astrological interpretation, for it is based upon observation and intuition, rather than 'animals in the sky'.

■ USING THIS BOOK

Reach Your Potential – Cancer explores your Sun sign and what this means in terms of your personality; the emphasis is on self-exploration. All the way through, hints are given to help you to begin to understand yourself better, ask questions about yourself and use what you have to maximum effect. This book will show you how to use positive Cancerian traits to your best advantage, and how to neutralise negative Cancerian traits. Don't forget that by reading it you are consenting, however obliquely, to the notion that you are connected in strange and mysterious ways to the web of the cosmos. What happens within you is part of a meaningful pattern that you can explore and become conscious of, thereby acquiring greater influence on the course of your life. Let this encourage you to ask further questions.

Some famous Cancerians

Ringo Starr, Diana, Princess of Wales, Meryl Streep, Franz Kafka, Amadeo Modigliani, Helen Keller, Emmeline Pankhurst, Amy Johnson, Donald Sutherland, Louis Armstrong, Ingmar Bergman, Julius Caesar, Jean Cocteau, Phyllis Diller, Ernest Hemingway, Henry VIII, Gertrude Lawrence, Anne Lindbergh, Gina Lollobrigida, Marcel Proust, Rembrandt, John D. Rockefeller, Nelson Rockefeller, The Duke of Windsor, Barbara Stanwick.

Naturally, the Cancerian tenacity, sensitivity and intuition are a tremendous asset in all walks of public life and the arts.

Caring, crabby, or just-a-bit-clingy – what kind of Cancer are you?

Here is a quiz to give an idea of how you are operating at the moment. Its tone is light-hearted, but the intent is serious and you may learn something about yourself. Don't think too hard about the answers, just pick the one that appeals to you most.

1. **Your best friend, or one of your children has come to you full of excitement, with the news that he or she has an opportunity to go abroad for six months. How do you react?**

   a) ☐ Smile and say 'How wonderful,' then your expression darkens and you mumble about the dangers of foreign parts. 'But of course,' you say, reassuringly, 'it probably won't happen to you.' In the following weeks you relay every news item about hijacking and kidnapping that you encounter, so he or she can be prepared for what's in store.

   b) ☐ You offer your congratulations and start to fuss about passports, suitable clothes, etc. Inside you feel a little hollow, and secretly wish the trip would be cancelled.

   c) ☐ You realise quite clearly that you don't want your friend or child to go, because you will miss him or her. Determined to keep this to yourself you do your best to give encouragement.

2. **You have agreed to accompany a lonely friend to an amateur opera/ school play/annual train spotter's convention. Now it's time to go, the rain's coming down in stair-rods and your car won't start. So you:**

   a) ☐ Just don't go – no one's getting you out in that! You settle in front of the fire with goodies and a video (once you got caught like that, chocolate all over your face, when someone you'd stood up came round . . .).

b) ☐ It sounds feeble to say your car won't start. You dream of excuses about ailing guinea pigs or incipient severe 'flu, but you call a taxi and go anyway. However, you have a good grumble.

c) ☐ You know it means a lot, so you go. Next outing will be to a nice restaurant, of *your* choice.

3. **It's celebration time, your birthday! Your favourite night out is:**

a) ☐ A night in, with one or two friends, bringing a take-away and a bottle of wine (their treat) – and presents!

b) ☐ You'd like to be wined and dined by your intimates at a local restaurant – with someone else doing the driving.

c) ☐ You don't mind too much what you do as long as your dear friends/family are there.

4. **A wonderful job offer arrives for you, with brilliant prospects. Unforunately it entails a spell in the back of beyond – the middle of a jungle! So you:**

a) ☐ Turn it down flat. After all, what about the mosquitoes! And the snakes! And what would you eat?

b) ☐ You embark on some really serious worrying. The prospects are good, but what if you get yellow fever? Oh, yes, you can be vaccinated against it, but what about the other tropical diseases? Who will look after your pets? What if the roof leaks while you're gone? What if . . . what if . . . ?

c) ☐ Wheel someone reliable in to cat-and-flat sit, pack half a chemist's shop and go.

5. **It could be you – and** *it is*! **Amazingly, you have won a large sum on the lottery. Now what do you do?**

a) ☐ Now you're secure for life. Drawing a blanket of investments up to your chin, you spend your time planning safer and more productive repositories for your money.

b) ❑ Wonderful! Now you can buy that dream house and leave all your worries behind. (Who are you kidding?)

c) ❑ You are thrilled to be able to buy the house you've always wanted and to care for your loved ones without anxiety. You are just as thrilled by your projects to build shelters for the homeless/a home for orphans/set up a College of Counselling.

6. **Your best friend gets drunk at your party, after having promised to help with the organisation, so you:**

a) ❑ Feel rather resentful that your friend has done this and is unavailable for you.

b) ❑ Fuss about with towels and advice. Eventually, you slip over in something disgusting. Why are people always such a worry?

c) ❑ Feel sorry for your friend, but really it happens to all of us at least once! You keep an eye open for your friend and stand ready with the fizzy white tablets.

7. **Love is:**

a) ❑ Security and ownership, 'till death us do part.

b) ❑ Merging and giving – never having to say you're sorry.

c) ❑ Mutual nourishment, give and take.

8. **Children are:**

a) ❑ A constant worry. First, there's the getting pregnant, then all the tests, then the birth – and after that, well . . .

b) ❑ A treasure. They should be seen and not hurt, and wrapped in cotton wool if possible.

c) ❑ A sacred trust.

9. **Your partner's ex phones at 2 a.m., pouring out a stream of abuse to make the receiver curl in your palm. How do you react?**

   a) ☐ Your patronising replies are oiled by pure vitriol (yes, I know you can do it!) You crawl back to bed but can't sleep. Next day a poison-pen letter arrives and the next the RSPCA inspector calls to investigate a report of cruelty to your hamster (you haven't got one). You retreat into your shell – how long will this go on?

   b) ☐ You put down the phone, leave it off the hook and snuggle back under the covers. Underneath your outrage, why do you feel this creeping sense of guilt and shame?

   c) ☐ You put down the phone and leave it off the hook. Next day you change your number. The caller is clearly unbalanced. You take steps to protect self and family.

Now count up your score. What do you have most of – a's, b's or c's?

Mostly a's. Well, at the moment you're a bit of a crab, it seems. Try to have a little more faith in life and be a bit less touchy. The world has a funny way of giving back what you give out – try a little trust, optimism and enterprise – it won't crack your shell!

Mostly b's. It seems you're a fairly average Cancerian – caring, sensitive and finding it hard to let go, move on. You can learn to make more of your creativity and less of your fears.

Mostly c's. There aren't many around like you. You are careful, but you don't worry over much. You are loving but never smothering. Remember that your warmth and capability can make some of us feel rather inferior – and let someone help you, sometimes!

If you found that in many cases none of the answers seemed to fit you, then it may be because you are an atypical Cancer. This may be because there are many planets in signs other than your Sun sign, or it may be due to the fact that there are strong natal aspects that frustrate your natural self-expression. Whatever the case, your Sun-sign potential can be realised. Hopefully you will find something in the following pages that is of help.

1 The essential Cancer

Just when we are safest, there's a sunset touch,
A fancy from a flower-bell, someone's death,
A chorus-ending from Euripides, –
And that's enough for fifty hopes and fears
As old and new at once as Nature's self,
To rap and knock and enter in our soul

Robert Browning, *Bishop Blougram's Apology*

■ PORTS IN A STORM

Cancers are the sort of people who will always be there to offer hot soup on a cold day or an umbrella on a wet one. They know just what to say when the damp is rising along with the mortgage and the dog's been sick. They also trot out a few phrases on occasion. Things like 'Waste not, want not', 'A stitch in time saves nine', and the eternal 'Be careful'. Cancers should be cherished, and their sensitivity should be respected. Cancers are worth their weight in Moonstones.

■ CANCER BODY LANGUAGE

Cancer people are not especially easy to spot by movements or posture, because, like all the Water signs, you possess the gift of camouflage. You won't sprawl at a dinner party or guffaw at a funeral – or if by chance you do, you are sure to call the next day, apologising. If everyone is dancing the Crab will join in, (but not always gracefully) and if talking politics is the game you will go along with that too. Cancers have a knack for settling themselves in the most comfy chair. Others will have to become as subtle as you Cancers are in order to locate you. When threatened, you may hunch or fold arms tightly over the chest. And there can be a certain 'sideways-ness' about you; some even have a lop-sided sailor's gait. But obvious you definitely are not.

■ MYTHS OF THE SEA AND THE GODDESS

Legends featuring crabs do not abound. The Crab constellation is Babylonian in origin, whereas in Egypt this star group was seen as a pair of turtles, or sometimes known as Allul – an unidentified water creature. For our purposes this last fact is the most telling. This is the sign of the Water Creature.

From water comes all of life, the Koran tells us. Biologists maintain that life on Earth originated in the oceans, and J. E. Lovelock, author of *Gaia*, puts forward the hypothesis that pollution of our seas may be more of a threat to global health than air pollution. All of us began our existence as a foetus, floating in a sea of amniotic fluid.

The Great Goddess

Many historians believe that worship of the Great Mother Goddess preceded other religions, and that in the Stone Ages She reigned unchallenged. From Her all life issued, and to the tomb, that was also the womb of rebirth, the dead were returned. All acts of daily life were seen as a sacred participation in Her Oneness. The Goddess was present in earth and sea and shone down in Her sister-self, the Moon, Queen of the tides. Many goddesses are associated with the sea: Welsh Rhiannon, the White Mare of the Sea; Greek Aphrodite, the

Foam-Born (Aphrodite was a powerful Middle Eastern goddess, trivialised in the Greek pantheon); and the Virgin Mary is referred to as Stella Maris – Star of the Sea. Connection between the Divine Feminine and the ocean runs deep in humanity.

The Great Goddess had a consort, who was born, mated with Her and died, as part of the seasonal cycle, to be reborn at an appropriate time the following year, son of his own fathering. This God paralleled the journey of the Sun from winter, through spring, summer, autumn and back to winter. Some mythologies place His birth at the Winter Solstice, when the Sun begins the slow return to warmth and vitality. Others place this event in spring. Later the God is cut down with the corn and begins His sojourn as Underworld King, until rebirth. Thus the Goddess is seen as the cycle itself, changing Her face but never Her essence, while the God travels the cycle as the vitality of Nature. Examples of this duo are found in many pantheons – for instance, Anatolian Cybele and Attis, Greek Aphrodite and Adonis, Sumerian Inanna and Dumuzi, and Egyptian Isis and Osiris/Horus. Such ideas are being revived by modern pagans, who feel the story brings Nature to life.

In time, a patriarchal consciousness usurped the old Goddess power, and She was demonised as monster or dragon. We are all familiar with the dragon-slaying motif. The best-known hero in this respect is St George, but there have been many others. The first was probably the god Marduk who slew his great-great-great grandmother, Tiamat, dragon-goddess of the primordial ocean in the Babylonian creation epic, the Enuma Elish. Such stories are, among other things, a metaphor for growing sense of individuality overcoming the collective and instinctual. We are apt to assume they depict the triumph of the 'good' and 'right' quite forgetting the lost values of the intuitional, the mystical – and, of course, the feminine. It is interesting that the phrase 'old dragon' almost always refers to some fearsome female.

What might this broad sweep of early mythology and theology mean for Cancer? Several important points emerge. First, the idea of Mother is strong in Cancerians, either through adulation of her, rejection of her or wish to embody her. Even male Crabs will embody motherly qualities in a masculine way – this is not the same as our traditional idea of 'fathering' which tends to be more stern and authoritarian. Male Crabs, with their protectiveness and solicitude are more accurately described as 'motherly' although, cultural pressures being what they are, many will hide this beneath a macho crust.

Second, where there is 'mother' there is 'child'. The Great Mother always has her Son/Lover. Of course, this is symbolic and certainly does not imply incest in a literal sense. For Cancer it means that the eternal child is also present within. Cancers have a playful, whimsical streak which can be fascinating and endearing and there is an unreachable quality to you – no adult can really enter the world of a child. And children can be strangely heartless. Occasionally, this can be seen in this most tender-hearted sign, when suddenly the chill of the deep seems to be rippling around one's ankles. Of course, children need protecting and nurturing themselves, and this is certainly true of Cancer.

Third, there is the ambience of mystery that comes in with the tides. We speak of the conquest of space, but we have no idea what strange and terrible life forms inhabit the Pacific trenches, thousands of fathoms below the surface. Cancer is a sign that senses many things that cannot be put into words. You are keepers of much instinctual wisdom that the rest of us have lost sight of. It is not easy for Cancer, who 'knows' and 'knows that he or she knows' but can't say why. It's all too easy to dismiss such matters as moonshine, and Cancer, not always being confident, may go along with this. However, intuitive Cancerians have access to wells of indescribable knowledge.

Fourth, we have cyclicity. The Cancerian nature ebbs and flows – yes, you are moody. No Cancer should expect always to be the same, feeling, reacting, behaving the same way, day after day. And yet you are creatures of routine, habit and security (or perhaps 'rhythm' is a better word than routine, for many Cancers are easily bored). It's one of your paradoxes. Like the Moon you are changing but constant. If it happens to be the Dark of the Moon, just wait. Soon you will shine, full and bright again. This gentle sign has boundless and complex depths.

◼ ELEMENT, QUALITY AND RULING PLANET

We have seen that each of the signs of the zodiac belongs to one of the Elements, Earth, Fire, Air or Water, and one of the Qualities, Cardinal, Fixed or Mutable. Cancer is Cardinal Water. The 'Cardinal' factor means that although this is an emotional and instinctual sign, most Cancers are quietly ambitious and secretly competitive. Equally quietly, and by your own circuitous route, you are often very successful in your chosen sphere. The Water Element means that Cancer is motivated primarily by feelings, but before we assume these folk are eternally awash with emotion, we need to look more closely at what 'feeling' in this context, really implies.

The psychologist C. G. Jung defined the 'feeling' function as evalu-ative and rational – yes, *rational*. We are prone to believe that the only approach that could possibly be termed 'rational' is the logi-cal, objective one, but feeling possesses its own set of values, its own sense, consistency and worth. Feeling people assess concepts, things, people, religions and philosophies in terms of impact on self, on human life, on culture, beauty, warmth and the bonds of relationship. Feeling people are in touch and in tune with the pre-vailing mores of their society. Cancer, like the other Water signs, is comfortable having a group with which to identify. This does not mean you lack individuality – far from it. However, a sense of com-munity and/or family is vital to you.

Nor should we make the mistake of confusing feeling with emotion. Cancers are emotional people, yes. Usually you are painfully aware of how you feel, but that does not mean you are necessarily driven by your emotions. From Cancer's point of view the tremendous advantage may be that if you know how you feel, or even how you are going to feel in a situation, then you have every chance of concealing these feelings! For self-protective Cancer this is a survival essential.

One last point, before we leave discussion of the oft misunderstood 'feeling function' – feeling types aren't intellectually inferior! Their minds do not necessarily operate with the detachment of the 'thinking' specialist. They do not usually ponder philosophy or construct a Lego skyscraper of facts, but they are very capable of making meaningful associations and often have good memories. Many fine doctors, therapists, writers and counsellors are 'feeling' type people, and there are plenty of Cancers among their ranks.

Cancer is the fourth sign of the zodiac. We began with Fiery Aries, the Pioneer, followed by Earthy Taurus, the Builder and then Airy Gemini, the Communicator. Now comes Cancer, the Homemaker, completing the first Elemental quartet. In the Northern Hemisphere the start of Cancer marks the Midsummer Solstice, when the Sun reaches its height and yet begins to 'die' as days grow shorter. This is a time of fullness, fruition, warmth and imperceptible change. Nature is lavish and fertile – Cancerian themes! However, in the Southern Hemisphere this is the Midwinter Solstice – time of the 'rebirth' of the Sun. In either case the leitmotiv of fecundity can be discerned.

Each sign is said to have a 'Ruling Planet'. This means that there is a planet that has a special affinity with the sign whose energies are most at home when expressed in terms of that sign. The Ruling Planet for Cancer is the Moon. Although the Moon is usually taken as representing the eternal feminine principle, there were many Moon gods and some cultures believed that it was the Moon god who made women pregnant and who brought about menstruation by having intercourse with them. We are more familiar with Lady Moon, mistress of magic, instinct, intuition and hidden knowledge – and these qualities have mostly been denigrated, along with the feminine, as the medieval witch hunts evinced! Astrologically the Moon indicates our reactions, habit patterns, gut feelings and instincts.

■ TIDES AND TRIBULATIONS

You Cancers are, in a word, moody! You can be very touchy, and your sensitive feelings may be wounded by a word or a glance, however unintentional. You may be asked 'What's the matter?', but getting it out of you is like dragging a lake. But if others do their best, they'll eventually get a glimpse of a smile through the mist. Soon all the Cancerian magic and charm will be back on land. However, it's a mistake to leave a Crab alone if you have been offended because you won't 'snap out it'. Oh yes, you may come round eventually, but that hurt will rankle like the foreign body beneath the oyster's shell. Sadly, what could result after years of this won't be a pearl but a thoroughly hardened Cancer, cruel side uppermost.

This is not to say that Cancer doesn't need some time alone, however. Time to reflect, dream and assimilate is essential to you. This sign is highly imaginative and creative, and you need the opportunity to envelop yourselves in dreams and moonlight. Mostly your imagination is positive, and even quite practical. You rarely go off on tangents like the Fire signs or get lost in the mystical, like Pisces. Your dreams have a certain tangibility and usefulness which may emerge in works of art, or in the creation of a most beautiful home. However, Cancers can often be found searching in the negativity drawer for all that could go wrong. You may become a prey to fears, which can take the shape of a nameless angst at a world that will never be warm and secure enough for your liking. Other terrors are easily named. Poverty is first on the list, along with not being loved, or even not having a Proper Home. A little further down the list may be illness, of self or loved ones. No one can turn a little cough into bronchitis, into pneumonia, into something terminal with the speed of an anxious Crab. However, Cancers are generally sensible enough to do something about their fears. Your enterprise keeps the roof over your head and the wolf from the door, and many a chemist's shop would be bankrupt without Cancerian patronage.

Perhaps the most surprising characteristic of this sign of surprises is your wanderlust. This is not the adventuring of Sagittarius, who will often go off just to prove they can. Neither is it the restlessness of Gemini or the impulsiveness of Aries. With Cancer it's an instinctual, rhythmic phenomenon – like the tides, it's just the way it is. Cancers like to rove and move, sometimes just for the feel of motion. You'll always come back – especially at dinner time – but you'll go again. Sometimes this is predictable and sometimes it isn't. This sign likes to pick up atmospheres from here, nuances from there. You like to see people and situations: it enriches your experience. A Cancer who has a secure home will be all the more inclined to rove, feeling sure of something to come back to – but Cancers all ebb and flow in more ways than one. It adds to your enigma and mystery.

■ CARERS AND CHEESE-PARERS

We have established that Cancer is a nurturing sign, in its element caring for friends and family. Generous, warm and sympathetic, the inscription from the Statue of Liberty 'Give me your tired, your poor . . .' could almost be incised on your brow (the chart for the creation of the United States, incidentally, has Sun in Cancer!). It is true this is the zodiacal Dr Barnardo. So, these people will lend an ear to the troubled, time to the lonely and give their last penny to a beggar. What? Now just stop right there. Did I mention money? There is a four-letter word for a certain side to Cancer – mean.

Of course, true meanness is a result of damage and denial, and a Moonchild who has received his or her fair share of nurture can be relied upon to give to any needy cause. However, Cancers are careful. Even those of you who are slow at Maths can still reckon up the interest on your account to the year 2010. And it isn't just money. Cancer is aware of value and potential value to the point where it becomes almost a figment of the active imagination. Crabs can find more use than Eeyore for an empty honey jar and a deflated balloon. This brings us on to another subject. Hoarding.

The Collection is an especially Cancerian phenomenon. In addition, most of you Cancers are hopeless victims of the 'shoe-box syndrome'. This means you throw nothing away, and I really do mean almost nothing. Somewhere in every Cancerian cupboard there is a cache of old shoelaces, torn labels, broken watches, dead matches and pens that haven't worked since primary school. Somewhere else there will be a trunk full of photos, love letters (and other letters), postcards, souvenirs and diaries. And in yet another place there will be a pile of frayed pillowcases, ragged flannels and handkerchieves translucent with wear. Get the picture? Throw it all away? Never! You never know when that old sock will come in handy. One Cancer described to me the feeling of trying to part with things. 'It can be almost like a physical pain,' she said.

It is not hard to understand the reasons for this. Roots and the past are deeply important to Cancer, and throwing away the smallest memento is like throwing away something that has formed one's own fabric. Hermit crabs make their shell from dead crustaceans and beach jetsam, and to many Moonchildren all these bits and pieces are a symbol of security. I say 'symbol' because Cancer is sensible enough to know that there is no real security in an old torch battery.

Like stinginess, excessive hoarding is a sign that something is, or has been amiss, and any Cancers who are thus beset are well advised to ask themselves some searching questions. You are wise enough to find the answers – and you don't have to tell anyone else!

▮ THE CRAB'S CLAWS

We have discussed tight-fisted Cancers and discovered the 'shoe-box syndrome', but on the whole yours is a charming sign – gentle, sympathetic, kind and loving. Your imagination is fascinating yet you are practical and enterprising enough to make something real of it. Although sensitive, you can be tough and are certainly tenacious. Besides a few eccentricities you possess all the ingredients to make a success of life and love – right? Yes, that is certainly so, but there is also another side to this sign, and it can be frightening. Those claws that hang on with such admirable dedication to what is of value can also be sharp and tearing.

We have seen that a sense of belonging and community is very important to Cancer, and in some this can extend to fear of being outcast. So Cancer takes her or his place in the group, and what defines a group, gives it its shape and organic consistency are the outsiders. Attacking the outcasts can just make some Cancerians feel more secure. Cancer will seize on anything different and mock it, because it is feared and envied. And in doing so Cancer can generate plenty of fear in others. This is a product of Cancerian clannishness and dread of being themselves an outcast.

Because Cancer is a 'feeling' Water sign, your thinking is not always original or even clear. You can absorb the half-baked opinions of your peers like a sponge and you Cancers are past-masters at the skilful put-down, backed with the weight of millions of 'they says' and 'everyone knows' behind it. 'She's no oil painting' and 'He'll never make good' are some of the lesser barbs. Underneath this occasional spite may lurk Cancerian resentment at needing others so much. Moonchildren have so great a wish to have someone to care for that it makes them vulnerable. They can become waspish at half the human race in self-defence.

The Great Mother had her darker side also. As well as supreme creatrix she was also the devourer – she took life as well as gave it. The Dark Goddess, the devouring mother can occasionally be seen in Cancer. This is how it may go:

Mrs Cancer's thirteen-year-old daughter comes in flushed and agitated. On her way home a man in a car stopped and asked if he could give her a lift. Having heard it many times from her solicitous mother that she should never accede to such requests she ignored him. Nonetheless, she is both excited and disturbed by the incident. It is the first time an adult man has shown such an obvious interest in her. Could it mean she is becoming sexually attractive?

'Do you think he just wanted to be helpful, Mum?' she asks. Mrs Cancer recoils. Could it be that the time is drawing near when her baby will leave the nest? Ignoring the plea for encouragement that she would generally have responded to with all her heart, the Dark Mother shows her claws. With a condescending look she replies 'I expect he was a friend of your father's dear. Go and tidy yourself up. I'll be dishing up the tea in a minute.'

It really is not hard to see how utterly crushing such a remark can be, especially if the teenage girl is herself a Cancer – but thereby hangs another tale. The fact that the mother in question would probably die to protect her daughter and unleash her claws in truth at any man that threatened her is neither her nor there – neither is the fact that our mother in the example phoned the police after the incident, the moment her daughter had disappeared upstairs. In fostering continued dependence, Cancer has just dealt a masterstroke, but it has been a sad move. Cancers need to be honest with themselves concerning their motives in such situations. The truth of the matter is that children who are encouraged, who have their confidence boosted and who are made to feel free are the ones who *always* come home, happily and repeatedly, from five to fifty-five – even if they aren't themselves Cancer.

◼ INTO THEIR SHELL

It is a well-known fact that a crab's only form of protection is its shell. Cancers also have their shell, into which they retreat to protect their vulnerability. This may be more than just a dark or unresponsive mood, which is easy to spot. It could take the shape of a variety of camouflages, where the Moonchild hides its true nature, and one of its favourite forms is a veneer of toughness or nonchalance. This is a favourite, especially with Mr Cancer. No one can play Mr Supercool better than a Cancer bent on hiding his sensitivity. It is not always easy for male Crabs in a world where 'men are men and women are glad of it'. Cancer, especially in youth, would rather give the impression that he couldn't care less.

Crabs love adulation and approval and they truly hate to be rejected or ridiculed. It is their great fear. Cancers need to remind themselves time and time again that if they do not come out of their shells and risk the glare and exposure, they will never find the nourishment they need, or the recognition. All Crabs owe it to themselves to open up, take risks – especially with their creativity – and reach out for what they need. It really is better that way. When you think seriously about it, what do you have to lose?

The cautionary tale (below) has relevance for many of us who have let our fears take hold of us and so turned something possibly unpleasant into something thoroughly so. It is especially relevant

The story of the Rabbit

North American lore tells the story of Rabbit, who was in the old days a fearless warrior, and his friend, Eye-Walker, the witch. These two were inseparable. One day they were out walking and Rabbit said 'I'm thirsty'. Lo and behold, Eye-Walker blew on a leaf, and there was water for Rabbit. Then Rabbit said 'I'm hungry' and food appeared in similar fashion. Rabbit ate and drank, but said nothing.

Later along the trail Rabbit fell and broke every bone in his body, but Eye-Walker healed him, with her magic arts. Still Rabbit said nothing.

They arrived home at length and Rabbit disappeared. Eye-Walker couldn't find him for day. When at last she found him, Eye-Walker said 'Why are you avoiding me, my friend?'

Rabbit cowered away from her. 'Because I am afraid of magic – go away and leave me alone.'

Eye-Walker's eyes filled with tears, but she said 'Rabbit, my magic has done you nothing but good and still you shun me. I could destroy you, but I will not. Instead I lay upon you this curse. From now on you will call your fears and they will come to you. Farewell.'

Now Rabbit is the 'fear-caller'. Out he bobs from his burrow saying 'Owl, stay away from me' and sure enough, down swoops Owl. He says 'Fox, stay away from me' and sure enough up races Fox. Those who have 'rabbit-medicine' are so afraid of various perils that they almost conjure them into existence.

for Cancer. Through worrying, Cancer may turn fears into a reality. This may not literally be the case – you can't cause a bank to collapse by having nightmares about it – but you can make yourself so miserable worrying that you might as well have lost your fortune anyway. More particularly, Cancers who allow fear of failure or ridicule to confine them to their shell are condemning themselves to certain failure. If you don't try then you certainly can't succeed. As for ridicule, no one may be laughing, but most important of all, deep inside, you will know that far from a comedy, this is a tragedy of wasted talent. I can only repeat – when it comes down to it, what have you got to lose? Only your fear.

■ PRACTICE AND CHANGE ■

- Your sensitivity is your strength. Never doubt this. Learn to make it work for you and do not repress it. There lies your wisdom and your knowledge of humanity.

- Remember you need to 'mother' something in your life, whether you are male or female. Male Crabs need not feel bad about this – masculine strength is touchingly valuable when used in a caring context. So whether it is your seedlings, your friends, your art, job, pets or wild birds, take care of them and feel blessed.

- If you catch yourself behaving in a mean way, ask yourself what you feel is really lacking in your life. Chances are that it is more likely to be love and attention than money or the clothes you wore ten years ago.

- Never feel ashamed if you are sensitive, fearful or cautious. It makes you more complete as a person but no less of an achiever. And what makes you think those loud confident types aren't hiding secret fears too? Bet you they are!

- Always turn time spent worrying into time spent doing something about it.

- If you are tempted to be waspish, always think how you would feel if you were the subject of a similar put-down. Although your friends may laugh with you they cannot be blind to the fact that you may do it to them one day. There is much more security in being fair to all.

- Say to yourself 'No fear' and 'Just do it'. If necessary 'Do it again'. Fortune favours the brave! *Feel the fear and do it anyway.*

2

Relationships

I wonder by my troth, what thou, and I
Did, till we lov'd? Were we not wean'd till then?
But suck'd on countrey pleasures, childishly?
Or snorted we i'the seven sleepers den?
'Twas so; But this, all pleasures and fancies bee,
If ever any beauty I did see
Which I desir'd, and got, 'twas but a dreame of thee

John Donne, *The Good Morrow*

It is said that there is no greater love possible than than of a mother for her child. A mother will do anything, sacrifice anything, even her own life, for her child. There is no closer or more blissful bonding than that of a baby, held in its mother's arms. Good mother love means always being secure, having emotional and physical gratification on tap, and enjoying instinctual communion with the love object; it means being 'one person', being needed, caressed and approved of – and it means forever.

It is a well-known fact that this sublime state is not enjoyed by all infants. Indeed, the possible dangers resulting from deprivation, when we are tiny and vulnerable, is well publicised in popular psychology. Cancers are often poignantly aware of the importance of childhood, and will not readily recover from any wounds they may have received. This love, which should be everyone's birthright, may not always be obtainable. Yet it is the quality of love, this totality and this bliss for which Cancer aims in adult relationships. Nothing else will do, and yet Cancer is sensible enough to know this sweetest fruit doesn't grow on trees. Small wonder the Crab is cautious!

Cancers do tend to 'mother' those they love – this applies even to the males of the sign, who can be gently solicitous. It is also true that Cancer can be fussy and demanding as any mother hen. However, it is the subtler qualities of mother love that really motivate Cancer, its beauty and symbiosis. Many Cancers avoid being the least bit 'mumsy', but when they give their heart they do so with total devotion – it is a rare and wonderful gift, so if it is yours treasure it deeply.

Moonchildren will often postpone the love thing. They procrastinate, dodge and deny. 'Why didn't you ask her out?' you may ask, having noted young Cancer's interest in one of the opposite sex 'Well, she could have asked me, couldn't she? I don't know her very well, and there's nothing to do around here. Anyway, I can't afford it – I've got to save for my car.' Excuses, excuses. Mind you, the point about money is doubtless true, for to Cancer money is the next thing to love on the security-requirement checklist. Of course, money is more predictable than love – a point not lost upon these people. Love comes first, but only when they are sure of it, and that may take a long time. Meanwhile Cancer will circumnavigate the love object in ever decreasing circles, checking things out and waiting to make a move. Some Cancers who have at some stage in early life been badly hurt, may endlessly postpone commitment because the very thought of it terrifies them. They may say they don't want to be tied down, but it is truer that they don't want to be let down.

Once committed, however, this sign is every bit as passionate and intense as its Scorpio cousins and just as private. Cancer wants, and gives, total commitment. Cancer likes vulnerability. In fact, Cancers will become hurt and deprived if others keep their guard up after Cancers have dropped theirs – if that should ever be possible. Cancer has a profound understanding of the emotions, and much is unspoken when feelings run deep. Having said this, Cancer can also express love in beautiful words. However, words are 'but puffs of air, blown from the mouth' and only the most lyrical poetry can come close to expressing Cancerian feelings. Better to gaze deep into each other's eyes and get lost in an everlasting kiss.

Speaking of 'everlasting', that's another important word when it comes to Cancer in love. This thing, which is naturally bigger than both of us, will last into eternity. One of the reasons for Cancerian circumspection is their utter dread of a break-up and many Cancers will endure the most bitter pain or live in a marriage that needs a decent burial, for many years, rather than face endings. Of course, Cancers do get divorced, but only as a very last resort, and even then they would often far rather manipulate the partner into doing the leaving. This means they at least hang on to home comforts, which can be no small consolation.

■ CANCER SEXUALITY

When the two-steps-forward-and-one-step-back routine has at last evolved into a lyrical *pas de deux*, Cancer can begin to relax and come into her or his own. In the glow of security, you blossom into one of the most passionately sexual signs of the zodiac. Moon-children can be deeply and ardently responsive, and for preference you do usually like to attune to the mood of your lover. However, this is a Cardinal sign, and Cancer is quite capable of doing the initiating once you feel sure of your ground. Cancer will play the entire cadence of emotional response, from savage, through tender, into playful and teasing and back to profound contact until both partners are engulfed in rapturous symphony. Sounds poetical? Well, it is of course, but what else would you expect of a Moonchild?

However, Cancer is no sexual athlete, collecting notches on the bedpost. Despite your sensuality there is often more than a streak of prudery in Cancer. The key to Cancerian sexuality, as with just about everything to do with this sign is feeling. Sex doesn't particularly interest Cancer for its own sake – although the distinction may seem a fine one in practice. Of course, Crabs can be randy, like anyone else. Their secret past often hides its share of one-night stands and debaucheries, because like all the Water signs Cancer has an urge to explore human experience – and that includes sexual experience – to the full. Some Cancerians have an interest in sado-masochistic pastimes, and there may be a *soupçon* of this in the most conventional of the sign. However, they do not achieve true pleasure without love, because it is only in an environment of acceptance that the Crab fully drops the guard and is able to explore their own responses. After all, you can't make love in a suit of armour.

Cancer will generously overlook the little foibles of a lover, once love is established. The Crab is tolerant, affectionate and realistic about human nature and sweaty socks. The soothing acceptance of this sign, the gentleness, depth of feeling and warmth make Moonchildren some of the best lovers – but there is a 'but' and it's a big one. You will close off if hurt or rejected, and your partners won't always know what they've done, unless they have plenty of Water in their own chart and are able to 'tune in'. Worst of all, Cancerians, like most emotional people, have often been taught to feel ashamed of feelings, having internalised the message that they might be 'silly'. This is compounded by the fact that it is so difficult to put certain things into words, especially if someone is demanding and probing. So Cancer goes quiet, denies there's anything wrong and all the shutters go up. It's like coming home to the cosy cottage and finding the lights off and doors barred. Love has moved out, and it's coldest of all in the bedroom.

This situation is by no means irretrievable, but it does need sensitive handling. The partner needs, gently and with great patience, maintaining receptivity at its height and demands to the minimum, to try to discover what it is that has upset the Cancerian partner. Believe me, this is worth it. Cancer may have imagined the slight, but more likely, the subtle sensitivities have been rightly, if somewhat excessively, stimulated. Cancers, on their own part, need at least to be prepared to admit that they might – just *might* – have got hold of the wrong end of the stick and converted a molehill into a mountain. Situations like this, if inappropriately dealt with, can develop into a relationship where the blinds are always drawn on the inner life, and that is a tragedy. If well handled, on the contrary, such episodes can contribute to a growing closeness and unparalleled understanding between the couple.

'The Dead Moon' – a folk tale from England

English legend tells of deadly marshes that plagued the county of Lincolnshire many years ago. On moonless nights ghouls and fearsome creeping things without name preyed on the unwary traveller. Hearing what was happening when her back was turned, the Moon decided to go down and investigate this dreadful place. She wrapped herself in black, from head to toe, so that only her bright feet could be spotted. But she fell, and her foot caught on something that tightened around her ankle, like a rope. She heard a dreadful wail from a man, caught in the bog, and struggled all the more, so that her cloak fell away and light beamed from her brilliant hair. The man found his way home, joyfully by her light, but the Moon was caught. The vile ghouls and monsters rejoiced at the capture of their enemy and pushed her under the mire, where the arms of corpses could hold her. They covered her with a great stone.

Meanwhile the people began to murmur about the whereabouts of the Moon, who had not shone for so many nights. All the evil things crept closer and closer to their cottages, and, in terror they

consulted an old Wise Woman. She gave them charms, but could not
tell them what had happened to the Moon. The people were at their
wits' end – until the man who had been caught in the bog the night
the Moon came down, suddenly began to piece together the events of
that fearful time. 'I know where she is,' he cried.

Armed with advice from the Wise Woman and all the weapons they
could carry, the villagers set off to brave the horrors of the bog.
While the ghouls and foul beasties moaned and whispered about
them, they hauled the stone off the Moon, so that she shone in her
full glory. Up into the sky she rode, lighting safe passage for her
rescuers. And that is why the Moon shines brightest over the marsh-
lands, for she knows what lurks therein.

This little tale has several metaphors for Cancer. First, like the
Moon, you do often 'shine' best when needed to protect others.
Second, Cancerian moods are often like getting caught in a deep
swamp. Mostly they are a personal matter, it is true, but like its
Scorpio and Pisces cousins, Cancer is aware of all the ills to which
the human heart is heir. The initial Cancerian worry or depression
can connect, as if by subterranean waterways, to loss and misery of
an oceanic kind. You can become depressed over 'nothing' but
often family history can be the avenue – for instance, a Cancerian
mother whose daughter is half-an-hour late may connect this with
what happened to Great Aunt Beatrice and imagine her daughter
dead and buried by the time she tumbles, laughing, through the
door with tales of lost bus passes and lifts with a friend. By no
means all episodes are so acute, however, and this sign can be con-
sumed by an angst that is hard to define.

Cancer must be treated gently at such times, and a calm, sensible
partner can do a lot to allay Cancerian fears, if there is also empathy. But Cancers also need to be aware when they have got

themselves caught beneath that old monolith, and to send out the rescuers themselves. Things cannot possibly look good from the bottom of a dank swamp, in the darkness. So roll away the stone, and rise and shine!

■ CANCER WOMAN IN LOVE

Along with her Piscean cousin, the Cancerian woman has been the subject of poems and eulogies on her gentleness, femininity and seductiveness. Certainly this is one of the most feminine ladies in the zodiac. Ms Cancer is rarely obvious. With a glimpse of lace and a waft of Chanel she creates her ambience, and it can be extremely sexual, if she so chooses. She may have a melting glance and an accepting manner that makes her lover feel it's okay to be – anything – silly, vulnerable, confused, passionate – and many men become a little macho in her company. Ms Cancer in love will do almost anything to please her mate. She will laugh at his jokes, console him in adversity and encourage him by positive words. In the bedroom she will be Madam Sin, in the lounge a gracious hostess, and in the kitchen – well, in the kitchen – there she's a queen. Most Moonladies know how to bewitch the palate and gratify the stomach to perfection. The phrase 'The way to a man's heart is through his stomach' should have been coined by a Cancer, but if not they all know the truth of it. Ms Cancer in love is Madhur Jaffrey, Delia Smith and Rose Elliott rolled into one.

These are cynical times and I hear you saying there must be a catch. Well, there is – or rather there are. That delicious package has a price. For one thing, Ms Cancer, once she holds her lover in her gentle embrace, will never let him go. Try to pull away and he will feel the Crab's claws. This lady doesn't give her heart lightly, or in a hurry, so he'd best make sure he approaches the relationship in the same manner. Through manipulation, scheming and by a ruthless practicality almost worthy of Taurus, Ms Cancer will hang on to her relationship and her security. This makes her a very dangerous Other Woman, should she so far compromise herself. This may sound like a drawback, but it is only so to the faint-hearted. If her lover is the passionate type himself, up for commitment and intimacy, then this is the woman.

The second catch is rather more subtle and destructive, and it does need effort and awareness on the part of the Cancer woman and her mate. Because Cancer is such a caring sign, living almost to nurture and be needed by others, Cancer may have a tendency to live her life through her husband and children – this may mean she prods them to achieve in ways that may not be of their choosing. The picture of contented domesticity has a subtler, wilder and more destructive side that can almost feed off the essence of those around. Some men react to this by pulling away, angrily huffing and puffing. Other succumb to the warmth and comfort, allowing themselves to be mothered and subtly despised by a partner who is secretly resentful. For how can a Mother Goddess be a goddess without a partner to match? The Son/Lover has become simply a son, and Ms Cancer becomes like the devouring Dark Mother, omnipotent and destructive, and rather more like a spider than a crab.

We have come a long way from cleavage and the smell of apple pie, to a place that seems quite sinister. Where is gentle, receptive Ms Cancer now? Well, she's still there, just as exciting, just as sweet. It has to be said that she needs what we might call a 'real man'. Someone who is secure enough as a person not to relapse into macho posturing at the first tweak of the strings, someone who can retain his individuality without destroying intimacy, someone who has the moral courage to encompass the emotional intensity but retain independence. Perhaps there are few such to be found, but a man who can meet Ms Cancer on her own ground, love her, care for her, be cared for in turn and challenge her where necessary is a man who has found, and provided fulfilment.

Before we leave the subject of Ms Cancer, we must say a word about Children, with a capital C. Of course, there are female Crabs who do not opt for motherhood, preferring to put their energies into other forms of nurture, but these are in the minority. To most Cancers, especially the females, children are deeply important. Love means children, as like as not. However, this doesn't mean that Ms Cancer is only too ready to dive into domesticity and stay in it, up to the neck. She may love her home, but rarely housework, and many Cancers like very much to go out to work. This is a Cardinal sign and Cancer woman will do much to further her own ambitions, where possible. Ambiguous, yet constant, changeable yet reliable, there are many facets to this lady.

■ CANCER MAN IN LOVE

If a woman has dreams of knights in shining armour or fantasies about gung-ho screen heroes, then she should give this man a wide berth. If, however, she values less dramatic qualities such as subtlety, sensitivity and loyalty then Mr Cancer has much to offer. In our times, when ideals of masculinity are being revamped, Mr Cancer might – just might – be coming into his own. Not that he'd believe it – he's much too cautious for that.

On first meeting this guy could be Mr Supercool himself. He may fancy a woman rotten but she'd never guess, unless she's as subtle as he is, and can deduce volumes from that shy smile. Mr Cancer won't sweep her off for a wild night on the town – not unless he has a generous dollop of Fire in his chart or she has expressed a definite preference for clubbing. This man would probably far rather talk to her and find out about her, her preferences, feelings and family. It is rare for Mr Crab to splash out on expensive gifts and meals, for although he has an appreciation of style – and he certainly loves fine food – he would far rather save for his own home, put money into his business, or just hatch his nest-egg.

Because astrology tells you this man is sensitive and caring, his lover should not expect him to wear his heart on his sleeve. Old traditions die hard and Mr Cancer may tell himself sternly 'Big boys don't cry'. Some will even strut the macho stuff, just to prove they can. Prizing feelings out of this Crab is like battling with a vice, so don't even try. His lover should show her own tenderness and vulnerability, and although initially he may stand back, afraid to be swept away by the current, eventually she should break through. Do not tease this man. If he loves you then he really, really does, and sooner or later he will tell you – then he may never give up. He is a great romantic, often whimsical, sometimes poetic – but he may be afraid of 'looking soppy'. His lover should give him time and only say 'Yes' if she means it. Like Ms Cancer, he won't let her go in a hurry.

To the majority of Cancerian men, Mother is important. If he makes this obvious, his lover should make sure she gets along with his mother, even if she's an old trout. Swap recipes, listen to advice and swallow your pride because this guy is worth it, and a man who is kind to his mother is usually correspondingly kind to his wife. If he doesn't talk about his mother that doesn't mean she doesn't matter, and if he eventually takes his lover home 'to meet mother' she should do her best to please. No, his lover doesn't have to sacrifice her individuality, she just needs a little tact, and if she's in love with Mr Cancer she'll need to learn this anyway – remember, he's sensitive. He may also see his mum as Wisdom incarnate and will worry if she find his lover wanting. A Cancerian young man who has not been well-enough mothered may despise his mother and make it obvious, but she's still important. Possibly he will hope that his lover will make up for this by giving him a little mothering, but if this is the case, beware! If his early experiences have been poor he may well have internal programming that states 'Mothers are bad' and then the lover is in a no-win situation. Of course, this is true of anybody, but it is especially true of Cancer, males principally, but the female too. If this is the case it does need bringing out into the open, sooner rather than later. The good thing about Cancer is that this sign is usually willing to look at feelings and where they originate, and will often earnestly work at relationships.

Never think this man is weak, because he definitely is not. Water is gentle but eventually it erodes granite. Mr Cancer has staying power and his own brand of guts. He'll avoid trouble if possible and he won't punch his rivals on the jaw. However, he's secretly very competitive and often goes off with the prize when no one knew he was playing. Once committed he'll stand by his lover, if she respects his feelings, mothers his children, his ideas and him (sometimes) and if she can also inject a little poetry and moonlight into the scene. He'll protect her when she's threatened, comfort her when she's down and prod her into action sometimes, too, when necessary. Who needs all that uncomfortable dashing about on white horses, when you can relax into the embrace of the ocean itself?

■ CANCER LOVE TRAPS

The Martyr syndrome

If things aren't going well in Cancerian relationships, this sign can well turn to emotional manipulation to sway things their way. All the Water signs are finely tuned to the emotional undercurrents, and often get accused of 'manipulating' when they are merely swimming in their natural medium. However, when manipulation is called for, Cancer can do it, and do it well. One of the most potent forms of influence is that of 'the Martyr' which Cancer can play to perfection. In its mildest form this can emerge as 'Well, dear, you just go off out again – I'm all right sitting here, listening out for the baby' (looks wistful). 'It's all I seem to do these days, sit here in front of the television – still you can't have everything – well, some of us can't. Do you know what time you'll be back, dear? Will it be after midnight again?' In its most potent form it can become a tirade, in the model of 'After all I've done for you' only put cleverly, so Cancer's partner may feel too bad about his or herself to get really angry.

If Cancer's partner can go out and have a good time after those sort of remarks, then he or she may well be a bit of a heel. However, some Cancers will not state their preferences and will expect the partner to guess what they want and force it into their closed mouths. When this doesn't happen, Cancer gets resentful and chips away at the self-esteem of all close by. Cancers can easily end up in relationships where they are being abused. Yes, they may well generate plenty of guilt, but that does no one any good, least of all Cancer. This can go on for decades with resentment piling up, and Cancer, in the end, almost enjoys the misery, drawing a sense of identity and purpose from their martyrdom – bad news!

If this is you, even a tiny little bit, then, simply, *stop* it. What do you want to do? Make a list. Where do you want to go, live, work, holiday? What do you want to be in life? I'm sure you do not want 's/he put up with a great deal' engraved on your tombstone, do you? The obstacles may be large but they aren't insurmountable, and Cancer is an active, if rather circuitous sign. You must leave someone else to wash up, mind the baby or collect the teenager, because you are taking care of no one if you aren't taking care of yourself. Leave behind the cosy mantle of 'Martyr' and have the courage to see what you can do – believe me, it's plenty.

The Limpet

Cancer finds it hard to let go, and once love has been declared, something inside Cancer flags up 'Forever'. This, of course, is all very well, and we know that 'forever' is the language of love. Sadly, however, it isn't always the reality, and we all have to learn to recognise when to let go and move on. But for Cancer this is supremely difficult. Because of this Cancer may linger in a relationship that is inadequate, destructive or even non-existent. A Cancerian teenager may 'moon' after an indifferent love object for many months; a Cancerian man may plan for a future with a woman who does not share his feelings; a Cancerian woman may stay in a home where she is beaten and degraded, rather than accept the four-letter word 'over'.

> Greek myth tells of the Moon goddess, Selene, who fell in love with the handsome shepherd, Endymion. Unable to bear the thought of being without him, she kissed him into eternal slumber. Somewhere, on a moonlit hill, legend says that Endymion still sleeps. Selene covers him with kisses, but she can never enjoy him, for he cannot respond to her or ever feel her kisses or her love.

There are parallels here for Cancer, who will hang on at any price, even anaesthetising self and lover, by manipulation, into sacrifice of integrity, individuality and true emotion, rather than admit that the sell-by-date is well past.

It is in the Crab's deepest nature to hold on, and generally that is laudable. However, all things have a season, and you Cancers must learn not to throw good love after bad. How can you ever achieve the fulfilment in a loving relationship that is your birthright if you waste your best energies like this? You may feel as if you'll 'die' if this relationship ends, but that just means you've invested a lot of yourself in it, and you can get it back, to re-invest. Believe me, you won't die, although for a while it may feel as if part of you has. And you deserve better. Make your plans, cut your moorings and set sail for balmier waters.

■ CANCER AND MARRIAGE

Of all the signs of the zodiac, Cancer is the 'marrying kind'. Slow to make a commitment, once this is given they take it seriously. Crabs are generally faithful, although naturally some do stray occasionally. However, they usually find their way back. Even if a Cancer decides the relationship should end, he or she would far rather manipulate the partner into doing the leaving than pack his or her bags. However, this sign does not take marriage lightly, and if the emotional intensity is sufficient, if there is caring, closeness and appreciation, it is most unlikely that this sign will look for affairs. If they do it's unlikely they'll be found out – unless they want to be. Cancer keeps a secret very well!

Children are often very important to both sexes. Many Cancerian women find their supreme fulfilment in motherhood, the only catch being that they may be so absorbed in the new arrival that the husband feels left out and neglected, and this is something to be aware of, for hitherto this lucky male will have been the sole recipient of the mother-love. Cancerian men are usually enthusiastic fathers, although they may feel sad and somewhat resentful that the little one takes so much attention from them. To many Cancers marriage means children, if not first and foremost then high on the list of priorities. It is important to this sign to have little ones to care for.

If you are a Cancer looking for a mate, you don't need me to tell you to choose carefully. What you may need to realise is that there aren't going to be any guarantees, however much you hesitate.

Life is always a gamble. Try not to anticipate trouble and go forward with optimism.

■ GAY CANCER

In general Cancer is a conventional sign, and so may suffer considerably if they realise they are different from the majority of their peers in something as fundamental as their sexuality. Many Cancers may try for years to squeeze themselves into a 'straight' role, when they are gay. Many will also enter marriage, in order to have children. Cancers who decide to come out, or at least to admit their preferences to themselves and select companions, need loads of emotional support, and a sense of gay community. They should ensure that this is in place.

'Straight' Cancers may sometimes find it hard to understand gays. The thought of being part of this minority, which is often poorly treated, may be quite frightening to them, and they may take refuge in condemnation. If this is you, you can do better than that! Society needs the emotional understanding of which you are capable – please give it!

■ WHEN LOVE WALKS OUT – HOW CANCER COPES

To Cancers the end of love is often a tragedy, and they may cope very badly indeed. Yes, you may find the occasional Cancer who is so tightly drawn into that shell and 'into denial' that little seems to happen, but mostly it's the end of the world and Cancer can't go on.

Fine! So you can't go on. Don't even try for a while. Let yourself fall apart, for a day, a week or even a month, if it's a relationship of long duration. Let it all hang out, but at the end of a reasonable interlude stuff your guts back in, get up off the floor and get on. I know it *feels* as if that certain someone was the only one in the world for you. This feeling may be so powerful that it seems as real as the carpet on which you're lying, sobbing into that handkerchief. However, I can assure you that what made this person so special was the emotional intensity, the dreams and expectations you invested in them, not some magical quality they alone possessed. Believe me, this is the truth and if you can't see it at least accept the theory. Draw all your available support systems around you. Go back to Mum for a while, if you so wish, or rely on your friends – but only for a while. Make plans to get out and get on with life; you know the saying about pebbles on the beach. You can live to love another day.

Starting afresh

The resilience of youth comes to the rescue of young Cancers, but for older representatives starting afresh can be a grind indeed. One of the problems here is that many Cancers tend to be 'very married', and if the partnership ends they have a hard time recovering their former individuality. After the first waves of misery and loss, many Cancers are quite clear that they wish to form another partnership, not merely to widen their circle of friends and interests. If this is the case, it is often a good idea to join a dating agency, for although this can be excruciating to some, there is at least the assurance that each person is after the same thing, which cuts through some of the Cancerian shilly-shallying. Cancers need to be very sure that they have emotionally let go of the old partnership as far as possible, so that new ones are not interfered with in subtle ways. Crabs also need a supportive network of friends and family to make them feel worthwhile and to make them laugh. A Cancer who is down may lose all sense of humour, but a good belly-laugh will do wonders to put Cancer back on the road to life and love.

■ PRACTICE AND CHANGE ■

● Give your loved ones room. Someone who is loved and also free will not feel the urge to break out.

● Remember to nurture yourself. So often Cancer gives away all the caring and solicitude, secretly hoping for care in return, and when this is not forthcoming resentment can set in in a big way. If you lie on the floor you cannot blame people for walking on you. Make yourself a promise that you will state your wishes and needs, and put some effort into getting them gratified.

● You may find that you are attracted to detached, cerebral types, and that they do not give you enough emotional closeness. This is not because they are purposely withholding – they really do not know how to relate in the intense way you do, but that doesn't mean they don't care. You sought their company to benefit in some way – try to let a little bit of that detachment rub off on you.

● Nurture some form of 'inner treasure' to help you cope when relationships go awry. Love does not always last a lifetime but your inner resources certainly will, if they are soundly built. Give some thought to what this might be, in your case – could it be an interest, a cause, a creative pastime, or even simply self-knowledge?

● If you do get into moods or are overtaken by fears and depression, don't accept this – it doesn't have to be. Be prepared to talk, however difficult it may seem. Make an effort to restore perspective in your life. If you are offended say so, rather than creating an atmosphere. Try not to waste time, but restore comfort and relaxation as soon as you can.

3

All in the family

East or west,
Home is best

Bohn

It is a rare Cancer indeed who does not love her or his home. Many Cancers have that domestic touch – a way of seeing to the small comforts of themselves and family – from quite a young age.

■ CANCER MOTHER

Cancer is certainly the most motherly sign of the zodiac, and many Cancerian women long, passionately for a family. Cancer's *raison d'être* is to be needed, and what more proof of your worthiness can you find than in a cuddly pink bundle, dependent entirely upon you? In addition, motherhood is a role sanctioned by society, and Cancer is often conventional. Cancer's desire for motherhood can be so intense that they will go to any lengths to achieve it. For a woman with a strong Cancerian element in her chart, infertility can be a life-rending tragedy.

Most Cancers are doting mothers, always prepared to stop what they are doing to 'kiss it better', leaving the housework (any excuse!) to get down and make animals with the Play-doh, setting aside the work they have brought home from the office to help with home-work, and generally putting themselves last. Cancer mother does tend to fuss a little and worry a lot. She likes everyone to have a good meal, or a nice piece of cake – homemade, of course – and is always available to talk to her children about their problems – up to a point. As the teenage years approach, this Mum may become more obstructive. Perhaps it is because she senses her birdies are flexing their wings, or maybe it is because her streak of prudery comes to the surface. Suffice to say that many Cancerian mothers can issue firm put-downs on teenage sexuality and become quite strict, where before they were relaxed and accommodating.

Mother Crab can become a tiger when it comes to protecting her offspring from dangers real and imagined. Don't bully little Johnny if his mum is a Cancer. Just because she's always had a smiling face and an open biscuit tin for you before doesn't mean you won't feel the sharp ends of her tongue, or worse, if you transgress. She's not above tackling other parents and teachers on fairly slender evidence if she feels her child has been misused – and she's not always open to reason. Cancer mother's devotion is wonderful, and in many ways she's just about as perfect a mother as you can get. Her only drawback is that she may tend to live her life through her children and the weight of all that love, attention and expectations can be a bit too much for a child at times. Still, remember that what she wants most of all is to be needed. Give her a cuddle and buy her roses on Mothers Day, and she may overlook the ring in your nose and ambition to be a full-time busker.

As this sign is so domestic you might assume that Mother Crab won't want to go out to work, but this may well turn out not to be the case. Of course, her motivation for living is almost always home and family, but she likes a career, too. She may forego advancement in order not to have to leave her family, but she has a mind that needs stimulation, and because her need for security is so great she likes to feel she is able to earn some money. This she will often spend on beautifying her home, and possibly hiring a cleaner. Being a homelover is one thing and being domestic is quite another – she'll often avoid dusting and vacuuming like the plague.

If a Cancerian mum is a bit strict or embarrasses her children in front of their friends by telling them to change their wet shoes, they should give her a break and think of all the times she's been there for them and remember that she worries. A quick phone call can do so much to ease her anxiety – and where would they be without her?

■ CANCER FATHER

Men are naturally more distanced from the birth process than women, but Mr Cancer, of all males, is usually the closest, and he'd get closer if he could. The whole idea of motherhood pulls at his heart-strings and fires his imagination, and he is often very supportive to his partner when she is carrying and giving birth – that is if he has received his own fair share of good mothering. If not he may get jealous, sooner rather than later. I even knew one male Cancer whose response to his partner's pregnancy was to have an instant vasectomy, and when she miscarried he was pleased. There may well be more to this story and his motives than I know, but it is entirely probably that he did not wish to share her attention with a new arrival, or make the transition from his cosy nook in the relationship to one of paternal responsibility.

Even the most mature Cancerian male may feel a few twinges when he sees the baby at his wife's breast and feels he has been pushed aside, and it is important that this new Dad is involved in the early childcare and made to feel loved and needed – not just as a father but as a man. This is important to all men, yes, but especially necessary to bear in mind with Mr Crab. All this notwithstanding, this man is a most protective and earnest parent, often very patient and caring. His sense of responsibility is lively and he will often become as deeply involved in the lives of his children as his other commitments allow.

Not all Cancerian dads are as demonstrative as they might like to be, secretly. Often the mores of the culture turn into voices that whisper things about manliness and stiff upper lips when they feel like having a good cry along with their child, who has just got 40 per cent in his or her best subject. However, times are changing and men are being encouraged to show their feelings. Mr Cancer can find a safe avenue for this – safer, that is, than admitting his own vulnerabilities – in entering into the concerns of the family. Mr Crab will often change nappies and wipe noses with the best. If not he will do his best to be the star turn at birthday parties and occupy a front seat at the school play, camera in hand. He may well be the father who ferries his teenaged children to discos and sports fixtures, reminding them about their jackets and money. There is no kinder or more protective father than the Cancerian, and if he's a bit gruff sometimes, well, that's probably because he's swallowing the lump in his throat.

■ THE CANCER CHILD

All things being equal, Cancerian adults are caring and often put themselves last. Yes, they may complain at times, but quite often, sometimes through their own fault, it is true, they do have something to complain about. Not so the Cancerian child. It has to be said that these often have whining down to a fine art, and, my! – don't they know how to get their own way!

It isn't that this child is not a charmer, for he or she may well have the most melting manner. Little Cancer knows how to please and is often sweetly affectionate. As time goes by 'making a cup of tea for Mummy' may well be the favourite pastime – did you ever think you could drink so much tea? However, before you become transfixed by the idea that this is a little angel, remember that all the Water signs are instinctive about human nature and very alive to the way in which their actions are received. I'm trying not to use the word 'manipulative' but it's no good – little Cancer can manipulate anything out of you, from that second lolly at age six, when you'd said, firmly 'No more sweets today' to that skiing holiday in Bulgaria at sixteen. 'But I'm not giving you spending money,' you hear yourself say, with that awful sinking feeling, as you reckon mentally what you have in the bank. No argument, or so you say, but your Cancer child knows better. The days and weeks go by and the hints fall thick and fast along with sad stories of the price of lunch at college and so you are inexorably manipulated.

We must remember that this is a Cardinal sign. Cancer knows what he or she wants and how to get it – it just might not be very up front. When your Cancer toddler monopolises the best toy at playschool, don't be surprised. Teacher may well defend the poor little darling from all comers, who try to get their turn, while Cancer manages to look pale and scared or screams loudly. Either way it's the same, and little Cancer may well end up on teacher's lap, at story time. Yes, these are sensitive children, but they are also determined.

This is also an imaginative and creative sign. These children often love fantasy. They don't usually like to play alone and may invent a playmate if a real one isn't available. Don't be afraid to say 'No' to little Cancer. They may look as if their hearts will break, but they won't. Just make sure that love and responsiveness are always on tap – that is what Cancer needs, and if they whinge about their wants and needs this may be because they aren't getting enough real attention. Be prepared to sit down with them from an early age and be available. Of course, all children need this, but Cancer needs to feel a rapport and to know that her or his feelings are a reality to you. As Cancers grow up, it is never a good idea for them to come home to an empty house, and if this is unavoidable make sure there is a phone number where you may be readily contacted. Cancer's day might have been tragic and they will need you to mop up the tears and talk some sense into them, or they may become morose.

Teenage years are dreaded by many parents. It seems to me that Cancer can go one of two ways. If they have not received the emotional closeness they require they may go into overdrive seeking intimacy elsewhere and that can well involve sex. Even Cancers who have received all the attention in the world may make themselves vulnerable. If this is the case then you may have to grit your teeth and pick up the pieces a few times. Try not to condemn, or lecture, but make every effort to show that you understand this young person's real needs and are not trying to spoil their fun or come between them and gratification. Never put them down or dent their body image, for they may never recover, and this will just give them more to prove.

Other Cancers are Sensible, from the start. They are aware of their vulnerability and they aren't about to expose themselves to any hurt they can avoid. And your Cancerian youngster can be mercenary – it's a form of security-building. Try to tell yourself it's healthy self-preservation when he or she sells old trainers for £10, but draw the line at HP agreements with younger siblings who are being persuaded to sell their souls for aged computer games.

Your Cancer, who might have been a demanding toddler and a wheedling adolescent, should, with any luck, evolve into a charming young adult who will value home, family and a good relationship with parents. A Crab who has been well treated is a Crab who will approach life well armed, and who will always find his or her way home again at regular intervals – because it's where the heart is.

■ CANCER AS SIBLINGS

Much depends on age gap and family position in the case of young Cancers. If there is a large age gap between Cancer and the younger one, the young Crab may well come into her or his own. Cancers respond to the little baby face and wipe chocolatey hands as if it was their own child – and Cancers make great baby-sitters (no, don't agree to pay for the service – do a little manipulating yourself and point out the many times you have driven here, paid for that, and remember the fact they want picking up on Friday at eleven-thirty . . .).

As a younger sibling, Cancer will probably get looked after by the older ones and will be seriously bereft if left out of their games. It is when the gap is small and Cancer is the eldest that you may experience problems with jealousy, and this will need to be handled with great patience. Little Cancers must not feel they have been supplanted, but neither must they steal all the limelight. In later years that Cancerian sense of family truly surfaces and Cancer is likely to keep in touch with everyone and arrange a gathering of the clans at festive times. Every family should have a Cancer aboard, just so they remember they are – a family.

■ CANCER IN THE HOME

We cannot repeat too often that home is mega-important to Cancer. Cancers love to have a space they can call their own, where they can establish their comfort zone and house all their familiar possessions. If feasible, Cancers should have their own room as soon as possible. I am not sure why it is that this sign, that needs intimacy, also needs space. Of course, Cancer is a deeply private sign, and so they need somewhere of their own where they can just 'be' away from prying eyes. Cancer needs to feel that the rest of the family are available for support when necessary, but does not want to live in their pockets.

Cancers do tend to hoard possessions, and they need space for this, although too much hoarding should be gently discouraged so they get into the habit of disposing of what is neither useful nor beautiful, nor a memento of anything very much. Ensure Cancer has a specific place for 'souvenirs' and for the inevitable collection of something-or-other that will evolve in time from teddy bears to videos.

Cancers are often quite clear about what they need for comfort and will arrange their living space to suit. This should be encouraged, for the young Cancer is learning to cope with and to satisfy their own needs. Often they are very sensitive to the harmony of their surroundings and may be very interested in the decor of their room – all of this is to be encouraged, and as soon as they become old enough they should be involved in choosing colours for paint or wallpaper and even helping with the decorating, where appropriate.

Making the best of cramped conditions

In my experience Cancers hate to be cramped, and this may be because of the violation of privacy and aesthetics that lack of space inflicts. If you really are short of space you must still try to ensure that Cancer has somewhere to be alone, when they so wish. If they must share a room, try to rig up a curtain to give them their own territory and make it clear to other siblings that they invade this at the risk of strong displeasure from you. Cancer will also need room for the 'collection' and this may need organisation. As Cancers get older they tend to become intensely aware of personal hygiene and clothes. A bed formed into a cosy nest on the top of a cupboard, murals that create an effect of space and depth, and soft lighting will do much to make a small space a romantic, private and well-organised one.

■ PRACTICE AND CHANGE ■

- If you have a Cancer in the family ask yourself whether this person is actually receiving enough attention. If not, take steps to rectify this, or your Crab will go into its shell. Sometimes Cancers can commandeer almost all the attention – attention within the family is an important matter for these folk. Ensure it is at a healthy level.

- If you are a Cancer, ask yourself where you can be more helpful, giving or understanding. You will feel good about yourself if you can feel that you are helpful and needed.

- As a Cancer you have a skill in keeping the family together. In some families this can seem a thankless task, but don't give up. You are needed, even if you do not feel appreciated. Keep making those phone calls and arranging get-togethers, and try not to feel offended if you don't seem to get a fitting response.

- Remember that however much you love your family and its members, you cannot live through them. Establish resources externally that can support you.

- If you are a Cancer whose family life has not been supportive, then do not give up. There are supportive and caring people out there. Look for a sense of community and like-minded souls.

4 Friendships and the single life

Old friends and old wine are best

Herbert, 1640

Friendships are naturally important to us all, whether we are in a partnership, or single. Naturally, those who live alone may have more time to cultivate friendships, but those of us who are committed need to make time for friendships, also. We may discuss things with friends that we could not with a partner, and it is more balanced to receive the points of view of several people. More than this, we do not get divorced from friends or have fights with them over alimony! A dear friend is one of life's greatest gifts. This is a fact not lost upon Cancer, although this sign may, sometimes have trouble making space, in a marriage, for friends, as they may become too devoted to their family. This needs to be borne in mind by Cancers who are in established relationships – friends will help them achieve a more balanced perspective and are a valuable source of affection and support.

■ CANCER AS A FRIEND

If a friend is needed who can be called upon in the small hours, to listen to woes sobbed down the phone, then this sign may well oblige. If Cancer has decided that someone is a friend they will go a long way towards understanding, consoling and taking care. Cancer will advise about garden and marriage, but they are more likely to be gently empathic than bossy. Unlike the more forthright signs, such as Leo, Sagittarius or Aquarius, Cancer doesn't really expect friends to take the advice literally. What really means a lot to Cancer is that their friends need them, and that they come back for more chocolate cake and sympathy.

Cancers are perhaps the most loyal friends in the zodiac – not that they won't have a bit of a giggle about friends behind their backs occasionally, or even allow a tart remark to pass their lips if a friend seems overly cocky, but they are nonetheless supremely kind. They will be there for friends, if they need them, and that is a great blessing. Cancer tries very hard to understand and to soothe – it's their nature. Of course, there is a limit, and even Cancer can get fed up with ceaselessly laundering wet blankets – remember, this is a Cardinal sign – they like to see some results, or at least perceive that friends are trying to help themselves. Occasionally there are subtle nuances that escape Cancer – they are orientated towards family concerns, relationships and feelings, of a fairly conventional sort. Although they are aware of the importance of moonshine, friends will get a very short answers if they try to combine this with money or security. Generally, however, there is no more perfect confidante than Cancer, if friends are crossed in love or have just spilt soup down their best suit, they will have advice and empathy on tap.

Crabs do like to keep their old friends and are quite careful about choosing new ones. Nor do they readily let anyone close – friends will have to prove their worth by time and understanding. However, once the friendship is established, these people will put up with quite a bit from their friends. They may complain, but they come back for more. To Cancer the devil you know is often far better than anything else that might lurk in the murky unknown, and while this can keep them in bad friendships as well as bad marriages, it makes for durability and reliability, and that is the stuff of comradeship. The only drawback can be the sheer possessiveness of the sign. Cancers don't like to let their friends go, and may be unconsciously influenced by the need to keep them close into giving biased advice – for instance, a Cancer whose friend has been offered a wonderful job that will involve living in town may make remarks like 'Oh, inner cities are so dangerous these days – think of the pollution, and the effect on the children. Are you sure you want to move away from the village?' What this Cancer really means is 'I don't want you to leave. Who will I have lunch with/ask to mind the kids/chat with over the garden fence?'

This caring Cancer friend who is always there for you will also want to be able to show you their own neediness. They will want to be able to confide in you their worries about their career prospects, their mother's illness or the ache they had in their left knee, and they will want you to sympathise and understand. Cancer really does relish a good moan. It is a great compliment to be trusted this far by Cancer, so treasure it. Crabs are also often great fun to be with – especially after a drop of falling-down water! They can be humorous, whimsical and pleasure loving, and they make marvellous hosts and hostesses. It is unlikely that you will be uncomfortable in a Cancerian home – so put your feet up, enjoy and reciprocate!

■ CANCER AND THE SINGLE LIFE

Of course, there are plenty of Cancers who have remained single, either through choice or necessity, but it is far more characteristic of this sign to seek commitment and security. Many single Cancers spend their time earnestly looking for partners and this may amount to a preoccupation, involving dating agencies and heart-searching discussions with friends, while the midnight oil burns, on the subject of 'How can I find a partner?'

However, the single life has much to offer Cancer, and those Crabs who find their entire *raison d'être* in looking for a permanent partner need to realise two things. One is that partnership is symbolic of security, of being wanted, loved, cared for – and that is all. Symbolic. A partnership will not necessarily give you these things, and if statistics are anything to go by, there is a fair chance that the reverse could be the case. If you are overly determined to find that special Someone then you may deceive yourself into believing you have found them, when you haven't, and then you will be in a far worse, more lonely state, that you won't find it easy to get out of. This is not to put anyone off who has found someone they wish to live with – it is merely a pointer to the importance of a little balance and detachment.

The second is that the single life offers you the opportunity to learn what is for Cancer perhaps the most important lesson of all – self-nurture. Learn to give to yourself and enjoy it rather than looking for someone else to give to, and hoping they will give in return. Yes, that may be the greatest fulfilment, but that road can be perilous. Instead, ask yourself what you really like – saunas, French wine, Chinese food, going to the cinema – and give it to yourself. Find a friend to accompany you, if you like, but do it. If there is a hollow space inside your chest, well, don't let that stop you. Some evening, when you have your feet up at your fireside and are laughing with friends you may wake up to the fact that the hollow has disappeared leaving a centre of warmth within that is your very own, that no one can take away.

■ PRACTICE AND CHANGE ■

- As a Cancer your gift is your loyalty, but try not to expect to own your friends.

- A good motto is 'Want a friend, be a friend'. Of course, this does not mean being a doormat, and we all know how much you do give. However, your friends cannot always be expected to 'rescue you'. People have different skills, and maybe your friends don't know how to be empathic, but perhaps they can make you laugh. Value your friends for what they can give – humour, companionship, shared interest – and take pride in giving what you know about.

- Be careful that you do not too readily write someone off because he or she seems unconventional, detached, cool or unreliable. That person may just be different, and you might benefit from their friendship.

- Always remember to look after yourself – do not expect friends to do it – they may not get the message!

- Friendships may offer you what a partner is less likely to give. There are fewer emotional issues and expectations between friends, as a rule, but loyalty can be intense. Do not sacrifice friendships in pursuit of permanent relationship. Your friendship may have more answers for you.

5

Career

The secret of success is constancy to purpose

Benjamin Disraeli

Crabs are tenacious and usually practical. In addition you have your own brand of highly imaginative creativity. These qualities are often in evidence in your choice of job or career, for Cancers usually finish what they start and are capable and resourceful. Cancers are dreamers. But while you dream you also plan. Crabs are much too careful to trumpet their ambitions from the rooftops, or to boast or demand, but you are good at insinuating yourselves into positions of influence.

■ TRADITIONAL CANCER CAREERS

The common denominator with most of the occupations suitable for Cancer is that they involve taking care of something or someone, or they involve the sea, which is traditionally associated with Cancer.

Cancer careers include:

- nurse
- counsellor
- historian
- antique dealer
- caterer
- businessperson
- financier

- boat-builder
- kindergarten teacher
- childminder
- housewife/househusband
- sailor
- museum curator
- caretaker

- estate agent
- hotelier
- fisherman

- market gardener
- archaeologist
- publican

■ WHAT TO LOOK FOR IN YOUR WORK

Many people have to take whatever job they can find – in a shop, in an office, or whatever. Only relatively few can choose a profession, train for it and find a truly fulfilling lifestyle, and as time progresses this is becoming more elusive.

To help you find a job that suits you, you need to bear in mind the spirit of what is recommended, not the specific occupation. One office job is not like another, one shop selling fashions may differ enormously from another in terms of environment and opportunity. If you are a Cancer you need to make sure of several things when seeking employment.

- There is an element of caring about the job. You need something to nurture and bring on.
- There is as much security as possible.
- There is scope for advancement through steady effort and creative thought.
- The money is good, and rising.
- There is generally an atmosphere of calm – few panics, unanticipated demands or looming deadlines.
- Someone is going to really appreciate your efforts.

There is no need to feel that you have to look for a specifically Cancerian job. Many Cancers would be bored to death in a museum or get seasick just looking at a boat. Look for something that suits in content and atmosphere, rather than its label. Be prepared to move on if something doesn't suit – however hard you plan, you cannot be sure how it will feel to work in a place until you have been there for a while. If you are unhappy or anxious at work you will feel ill. Make sure your job looks after you.

▣ THE OFFICE MOANER

Some Cancers go into negative mode and get swallowed up by a deep-sea persona called the Moaner. These people have about as much sparkle as a Pacific trench but their resourcefulness in finding something to complain about is unparalleled. They moan about the new boss, the old boss, the computer system, the new recruit, the size of the salary and the lunch-break, the workload, the new routines – and so it goes on and on and on. The Moaner especially likes to hold whispered dialogues in the toilet, or make tart comments, including you in them with a knowing wink.

The Moaner may seem harmless enough, but make no mistakes, this person is dangerous. Here we have Cancerian sensitivity turned to resentment, ambition turned destructive, imagination on a negative trip, and the nurturing qualities subverted into a subtle force that will undermine everything. The dangerous thing about the Moaner is that the complaints are seductive. We all have resentments, we all love to give them a stir and watch them boil and bubble – this is called letting off steam. There can be a wicked satisfaction in the verbal shredding of rivals, and the Moaner can be very funny on the subject of everyone's foibles.

The Moaner is a sad creature who feels deeply hard-done-by and finds solace in destructive comments. The Moaner isn't necessarily scheming to get others out of the way, the Moaner just likes to feel that others are with them in their dissatisfaction, and while the Moaner is clever enough to avoid detection by those higher up the scale, he or she rarely makes it to the top. The best way to deal with the Moaner is to refuse to be drawn in. Respond with an airy laugh, or try saying 'Come on, get a life – it's not that bad'.

■ SINCE NINETEEN-HUNDRED-AND-FROZEN-TO-DEATH

Cancer is an ambitious sign, but there are certain Crabs who, through bad luck or excessive caution, have been overlooked. These may relapse into the negativity of the Moaner or they may find solace in Knowing Everything. Many Crabs have formidable memories, and this one, who has been here so long they built the block around him or her, remembers everything from office gossip to the complexities of each customer account – from two generations back. With a memory like a CD Rom it really doesn't matter that this Crab shuns the computer, for one is hardly needed. Such a character is a favourite for mickey-taking, but that is a shame. Frozen-to-death probably has a quixotic sense of humour and a fund of wisdom about human nature that comes from watching so many people come and go, with knowing eyes. He or she probably knows several tricks for getting round those in authority and generally keeping people happy. Take him or her out to lunch – don't expect this Crab to pay – and give him or her a chance to thaw in the Cancerian glow of a hearty plateful. It could be interesting!

■ THE CANCER BOSS

This boss may be quiet, possessing a gentle manner and an air of tolerance. He or she may remember an employee's birthday and know how long, to the day, that the employee has been with the company. Often the Cancer boss may say to an employee 'How are you?' Just as often he or she will stomp in glowering, and if that happens, best stay away. It is at times like this that employees realise this boss isn't a pushover, by any means. Sometimes this person may seem a sentimental soul – the desk of often covered with family photographs. However, if you let your Cancer boss down you will be out on your ear in a most unsentimental fashion. There is a trace of ruthlessness in all the Water signs, and it is present in ambitious Cancer.

If you are a Cancer boss you aren't easy to impress, and employees may play on your Cancerian sympathies only so far as they don't jeopardise your position, or until you realise what they are doing. Either way that doesn't give them very much rope. You will like it if they remember your birthday, or those of your children and will appreciate a cup of tea – and a piece of cake, if there's one going. Yes, you do respond to consideration, but only so far.

No amount of solicitude will make up for lack of employees' commitment to their work, however. And then there are the inevitable Cancerian moods that sometimes make them wonder what on earth they did to get their heads bitten off like that. Don't worry, it probably wasn't anything, and this sign, that forgets nothing else, may well forget that bad mood later in the day. Employees shouldn't respond by getting in a mood themselves, for Cancer may take it personally.

You aren't always an easy boss to cope with for it is hard for employees to know where they are with you. Some Cancers do keep up an almost unfailing geniality, while others keep a similarly durable grim mask. Either way, what employees see isn't what they get. However, pleasing this boss is actually very simple, if employees have the human touch, gentleness and a smile, don't get into bad moods too often and work hard and diligently. That should keep you happy, and with any luck your employees will be with you on that circuitous route to the director's chair.

■ THE CANCER EMPLOYEE

At the interview this person may seem diffident and lacking in confidence – alternatively he or she may put up a bright-and-breezy smokescreen. Possibly an employer may find Cancerian interviewees hard to size up. They shouldn't be underestimated. The employer should feel complimented that they have applied to him or her for a job. Cancer is usually cautious and does little without a purpose. If Cancers decide that they would like to work for an employer it could mean that that employer is part of their Life Plan. For a variety of reasons this makes Cancers a very good catch indeed.

Roots in the past, Cancerians none the less have an eye to the future – nothing to do with sci-fi, but everything to do with paying off their mortgage by the time they are thirty-five. Believe me, this isn't an exaggeration. I know a high-spirited sixteen-year-old who is adamant that he will never have a credit card and will own his own house, lock, stock and barrel, before the mid-life crisis (which he aims to avoid). From the look of his bank account, he may well achieve this. Needless to say, he was born under the sign of Cancer.

If an employer decides to employ a Crab the chances are that this will be a worthy catch. This person can gently charm the clientele. Often Crabs are past-masters of the 'soft sell'. They do not like to foist the unwanted on the unwilling, for they are too sensitive to the feelings of others. However, they enjoy giving a service and can be uncannily accurate about the needs and trends of the public in general and the particular customer. These people have a rare combination of creative imagination, reliability and tenacity. They have an instinct for value and a good memory for faces. Usually reliable, they have consideration and determination. Crabs, as we have seen are ambitious. Do not make the mistake that, because their demands are often quiet they can be fobbed off, because if they are not satisfied they will leave – possibly not this month or the next, but nothing is going to stand in the way of Cancer for very long.

To get the best out of Cancerian employees, employers should not make sudden demands or changes. Give them time to adjust – they don't take long, but they cannot adapt instantly. They need to manoeuvre themselves back into a position where they feel they have some control. Neither should they be expected to work in an atmosphere of discord. If they appear upset, give them a few minutes to talk about it. They may not give much away, but they will appreciate it and the reward will be extra loyalty and commitment. Always show appreciation – Cancer needs praise. Listen to their creative ideas, for they may be well thought out and very workable. For goodness sake, pay them as well as possible, and promote them where appropriate; that retentive memory, that commitment, that imaginative flair should not be lost to the opposition.

■ WHEN UNEMPLOYMENT STRIKES

This sign is the uncrowned monarch of angst, and unemployment can worry the most casual of us. Small wonder that Cancer may be driven to the point of nervous breakdown by this threat to security. Cancers are often skilful at avoiding this eventuality, having sensed what was coming with their intuition. Many Crabs have alternatives set up in place, 'just in case'. Occasionally there may be a Crab who welcomes the freedom. Mostly, however, Cancer worries more than anyone when out of work.

This is when Cancer needs her or his faith in life more than any-thing – that knowledge that the tide that ebbs also flows, inevitably. One bonus about being off work is having extra time to spend at home, which Cancer often enjoys heartily. If you have lost your job, tell yourself not to panic. You are allowed one night of escapist indulgence, and then you have to get back on the track of work. Note your assets, which are probably people skills and old contacts. Look up all the names in your address book. Call each of them – there are probably quite a few – and let them know that you are in the market for a new job. One thing that you must not do is relapse into depression. It is absolutely certain that you can get out of this if you keep your spirits up.

■ SELF-EMPLOYMENT AND OTHER MATTERS

Not all work relies on a company and an employer, for there are many other approaches. Cancers often have an excellent, formidable business sense, and they are usually good at networking, keeping in contact with a variety of people and remembering what makes them tick. They usually have fat address books, bulging with contacts. Cancers often have a tough, independent streak and they may not like to give their creative designs to anyone else. In addition, they have a way of descending into the waters of the imagination and bringing back a trophy to dry land. What this trophy is will depend upon the talents of the Cancer, but it could be anything from a painting to a brilliant business plan. All of this makes Cancer a good candidate for freelance work or self-employment. However, there is one drawback – yes, you've guessed. Cancer tends to worry. Independent Cancers shouldn't take too many risks (as if they need telling!) for it may be too stressful. Also an optimistic partner who has a talent for setting the Crab's mind at rest is a great advantage.

■ PRACTICE AND CHANGE ■

● Remember, when selecting employment, there has to be an element of nurturing. This is conceptual rather than actual, for stocks and files don't need 'nurturing' like plants or people. However, you must feel needed, you need to watch something grow and you need to feel creative.

● Do not subject yourself to stressful environments. Seek people who are positive, a work environment that is well ordered and calm.

● Sometimes you need to remind yourself to be more direct, or you may miss that opportunity.

● If you are feeling stale do not allow your fear of the unknown to block the path to change – fear of the known is far worse. In this case the 'known' is frustration, lack of recognition and probably lack of money. What unknown could be worse than that?

● In your plans for security and advancement always build in room for your own creative imagination. You may not sufficiently value this.

● Your family may accept and understand your moods, but you can't expect those you work with to do the same. Do you really want people to think of you as cantakerous and moody? Will that help you on your way? Decide that you will be as sensitive to the feelings of others as you are about your own.

● Always remember, in your working life negativity is not an option.

6 Healthy, wealthy – and wise?

Wealth is not without its advantages and the case to the contrary, although it has often been made, has never proved widely persuasive

J. K. Galbraith, *The Affluent Society*

HEALTH

Astrological reflections on health are not always helpful, for health is influenced by a variety of factors that often have nothing to do with the Sun sign. However, from the general temperament of Cancer we may discern some useful pointers.

Cancer is an emotional sign, so you Cancers have strong needs and a high degree of sensitivity. Family or personal matters may prey on the Cancerian mind. You sense the undercurrents and the unspoken needs of those around you and may respond to this by feeling stressful – you often take the provision of everyone else's emotional requirements upon your own shoulders, and then your own needs go a-begging. Of course, Cancer hopes that concern for others will be reciprocated, but often it isn't, leaving you with a store of resentment and unmet requirements. The effect of this on your health may be twofold.

First, it is healthy to have certain basic needs met. One of these 'basics' is to feel that those around us care for us and have us in their thoughts. Research has shown that cuddles really are therapeutic. Second, Cancer does tend to find compensation for the affection that might be withheld, but this isn't always in a healthy way, such as overeating, smoking, drinking too much alcohol or endless cups of strong coffee. Generally, Cancers do need to be very open with themselves and others about what their real needs are, for the drawbacks of substitutes are all too obvious. You need to reach out and take what you need, and if you are in a situation where this is really not forthcoming, get out and find it elsewhere.

Of course, plenty of Cancers are good at wheedling what they want out of everybody, but even these may just be saying 'Love me. Make me feel really special.' Anything else is a sop, and may be bad for health, teeth or pocket.

The other problem with Cancer is often worry. You are imaginative people who may frighten yourselves into the jitters, disappear into a pool of self-pity or merely find it hard to smile, because that weight on your shoulders seems to drag at the corners of your mouths. Worry can mean all sorts of things from insomnia to ulcers. What is most therapeutic for Cancer is a good belly-laugh.

Having said all of these things, Cancer is often a very resilient sign; while you may appear sensitive, you somehow manage to recover quickly and display an innate toughness.

Stomach and digestion

Cancer is said to rule the breasts and stomach, and some astrological texts state that women with Sun in Cancer tend to have a large bustline! More prevalent among Cancers is a tendency to pre-occupation with the digestive tract and intermittent 'tummy troubles'. When Cancer is worrying about something, there may be inevitable stomach ache, or even nausea. The gut readily responds to the emotions, and Cancer may exacerbate this by comfort eating, or drinking. Cancers who feel stressed out should make sure that they give themselves a 'treat'. One of the best treats may be a massage with essential oils – perhaps lavender or lemon balm.

Cancer is ruled by the Moon and women of the sign may be especially conscious of water retention at the time of their period.

■ MONEY

We have already observed that you Cancers like to hang on to your money. Some Crabs are fairly impractical about expenditure and cost of living, and this may be because they are manipulating someone else into doing the 'caring' in this respect. However, they always get good value for what they do spend. Crabs who feel denied may go out and buy themselves a little 'something' to compensate, or they may give in to the demands of loved ones, against their better judgement. Mostly, however, their motto could be 'Look after the pennies and the pounds will look after themselves'.

Young Cancers may like to get a job as early as possible, if only for weekends or after school. Babysitting is something they are often very good at. This is to be encouraged. Cancer needs to be taught to develop a good budgeting system, for birthday presents and Christmas presents do need to be bought, and the sooner the young Crab realises that not all the money can be stashed away, or spent on their favourite food the better. Finances are about ebb and flow, and Cancer needs to become acclimatised to letting go, when appropriate. Mature Cancers usually are fairly good at managing finances, although moods of indulgence do overtake them at times. Cancer feels safest when the bank account is healthy, the insurance is in place and the money comes in with a regular flow.

To help themselves Cancers need to remember that comfort buying, as with comfort eating, is counter-productive. It just gives you something additional to worry about, such as poverty or obesity. Crabs must always ask themselves whether that special purchase is really going to give them the satisfaction they need, and if so for how long? If you need a fix, look at the balance on your Building Society statement – never mind the juicy steaks and Gucci shoes. And if you are reluctant to pay out when you know that must be, then you are becoming financially constipated – not healthy. Trust in the universe. Relax and visualise waves slowly rising and breaking on the shore. As the tide goes out, so it will come back in – go with the flow!

■ WISDOM

Cancerian wisdom is the wisdom of the heart. Cancer knows what human beings need. Their instincts are powerful and often un-erringly accurate, and their common sense is pure gold – when applied to other people that is. You Crabs are not always good at practising what you preach, but you know, deep inside, how things are and what the truth of any matter may be. Like the other Water signs, Cancer will often say 'I've got a feeling' and when they begin like that, you better listen. Male Crabs may be less likely to trust this side of themselves, but they are potentially just as gifted. Cancerian wisdom may also be of the day-to-day practical variety, and their homilies about cooked meals and early nights are worth noting. The Cancerian combination of empathy and common sense, put into words and beginning with a brisk, yet gentle 'Come now, dear' may be one of the most reassuring things you will hear. Cancers need to listen to their own hearts, to their own common sense and to respect their own wisdom – it's priceless.

■ PRACTICE AND CHANGE ■

Health

- Ask yourself what unhealthy habits you have acquired. What are they a substitute for? Decide what changes you will make, wait for a day when you feel good, and launch your new way of being.

- Some Cancers 'punish' themselves for their bad habits, feeling guilty and worthless. This just sets up a cycle of need and deprivation. A classic example of this is food binges followed by stringent dieting. Dieting slows the metabolism, which just makes it harder to lose weight. Exercise, on the other hand, speeds the metabolism and increases muscle tissue, which increases metabolic rate. Cancers should aim to take regular, pleasant exercise of a type they enjoy, and eat healthily, but enjoyably.

Wealth

- Realise that money will not bring you emotional security. Nurture enough faith in yourself to assure you that you will be able to replenish your money, if you have to spend a large amount.

- If you are a Cancer who avoids financial realism either because you prefer someone else to do the worrying or because you are just too afraid to know, ask yourself if you are really secure about this? You owe it to yourself to have some idea of what is going on, for many things can happen in life. You will feel far better if you have a clear idea of incomings and outgoings.

- Always listen to your own 'still, small voice'. It has the wisdom of the ages in it.

7

Style and leisure

The Owl and the Pussy-Cat went to sea
In a beautiful pea-green boat.
They took some honey, and plenty of money,
Wrapped up in a five pound note.

Edward Lear, *The Owl and the Pussy-Cat*

■ YOUR LEISURE

Many Cancers find it hard to relax on their own – they like companionship. It is true that they may be in dire need of some space of
their own, and may actively seek solitude when in one of their
'moods'. However, sooner or later Cancer realises that enjoyment
wears rather thin unless it is shared. If you are a typical Cancer it
may be quite hard for you to give yourself what you need without
the endorsement of someone else. Cancers may feel that they
should be somewhere else, doing something else, instead of relaxing. Seeking the company of like-minded friends will ease this
somewhat, for there is 'safety in numbers'.

We have mentioned several times that Cancer is secretly competitive.
Many Cancers enjoy sport – and they may not be good losers! They
do not usually like to push themselves to the limit for they are
rarely interested in proving the lengths to which their bodies will
go, unless this has somehow got mixed up in their minds with the
urge for security. However, they like to feel capable and can be quietly
smug when they win. Any competitive game can appeal – games
such as tennis that can be played in doubles may be preferred.

Martial arts are sometimes a favourite – these appeal to the Cancerian need for security, defence and to be 'one jump ahead'. Traditionally, Cancer is also linked to the sea, water and water sports, and it is true that all such pastimes are very relaxing, generally.

Recreation that is physically soothing can be very good for Cancers. This includes aromatherapy, massage, saunas and the like. These all send messages to the brain about security, comfort and approval, and Cancer is always hungry for these. Crabs often enjoy going to exhibitions or shows if some article that they collect is being displayed. Their interests cover a wide range, from vintage cars to embroidery, but it has to have a personal meaning. Some Cancers are very interested in history and can have great fun researching the family tree, exploring their locality for relics of bygone times or visiting stately homes. Many Crabs are excellent gardeners and will derive huge satisfaction and solace from their plants and from being with growing things. Equally they are usually splendid cooks and may while away happy hours – without any guilt – making something mouthwatering for friends and family. However, they are less keen on the washing up! Certain Cancers may take pride in a cellar full of fine wines, and you will usually find that somewhere, somehow, there is a Collection – stamps, china, old 45s – in which the Cancer takes great pride.

Cancerian pastimes are not likely to be whacky, unless there is a large helping of Fire or Air signs in the chart. Cancer prefers to indulge in pastimes that are socially acceptable to her or his peer group because this makes them feel more comfortable, more a part of something. Possibly what does Cancer the most good of all is a jolly good laugh. All Cancers should make a point of associating with people who can make them laugh, going to shows, watching videos – anything that will take them off into a prolonged giggle – it does them the power of good.

Holidays

Cancer loves holidays! This home-loving sign also has a great urge to take to the open road at regular intervals. However, it is hard to escape the nagging feeling that all is not well – and then, of course, one has to come back! A Cancer who is happy at home loves coming home almost as much as setting off!

If you are a Cancer, comfort on holiday is probably very important. Some Cancers like caravanning, because this appeals both to their sense of adventure and familiarity – they are almost literally like crabs then, with their house on the back! Boating holidays can be good fun, as long as they are not too much like hard work. Generally a nice hotel is by far preferable, and if there is a view over the ocean so much the better. There should be sports facilities on hand and other forms of entertainment. Needless to say, the food should be excellent and the beds comfortable.

On holiday Cancer does not like to be bored. A few days lazing in the sun may be fine, but Cancer will like to see something of interest. Local history, perhaps or local crafts.

Of course, a holiday is not just for the time spent away. Cancer will derive much pleasure from planning and dreaming.

■ YOUR STYLE

As a Cancer your style is generally one of comfort and quality. Again you do not like to depart too much from the mainstream, and this may mean that you insist on the fashionable, although you aren't likely to set trends yourself. You are very aware of the effect your appearance may create. Clothes must be comfortable, but they must also be of good quality and you are keen on a few designer labels if you can afford these. Sometimes you will like to be formal, at others casual, and you will need to cater for both these modes. Most Cancers feel happier with soft outlines, soft fabrics that drape and colours that are subtle and muted. Shades of blue and green often appeal, with silver the favoured metal. Female Cancers are usually very feminine, perhaps favouring floaty clothes and floral perfumes. Male Cancers tends to be conventional or relaxed, in a sporty way.

Crabs seem to need plenty of space – possibly this is because they collect so much stuff around themselves. Traditional furniture will probably appeal, and that is often built on a queenly scale – solid wood, with glass cabinets for display and shelves to house the family photos. Cancers need lots of drawers and nooks for their bits and pieces. Cosy corners, warmth, homeliness and tradition are the Cancerian style, with space for objects of beauty, portraits and art-works executed by the Cancer and other family members. This home should feel like home.

When you are choosing purchases for yourself or your home think comfort, familiarity, tradition, beauty, security, privacy, quality, timelessness, durability. Bear in mind fashion when choosing clothes – you will not want to be behind the times. Tradition is for your living space, not your wardrobe. Generally you will think fairly carefully about what you buy. If you really like something or find it fits exceptionally well – for instance, shoes – buy several pairs. However, do not buy too many, for you won't be able to wear them all out before the fashion changes. Make sure that you have sturdy hangers, shoe trees and plastic bags to cover special items in the wardrobe – you like to look after your clothes. A clothes brush and shoe polish are a 'must'.

■ PRACTICE AND CHANGE ■

- I know how you like to keep things but you need to be stern with yourself once in a while. You can't possibly enjoy anything or even find anything if you are choked up with the grot of ages.

- There isn't any point keeping clothes that are now too small for you. Yes, I know that you are going to lose weight – and when you do you'll want a lovely new wardrobe, not all that old stuff. Shunt that off into a siding, pending final departure.

- Romantic colours probably suit your personality best, and if you like blues and greens then it is possible to find a shade that suits you. If you have bought clothes that are garish or too formal because you thought you 'should', then ask yourself if you have ever felt good in them. If not – out!

- Ask yourself when you last had a really good time? Isn't it time you planned another?

- Review a typical week. How much time in your schedule is devoted to you, just you? Chances are that it's not enough. Decide that you will set aside an hour each day for yourself, perhaps soaking in a scented bath, surrounded by candles, with a glass of wine by the taps.

- What plans do you have? You need something to look forward to, not just for stimulation but also for security, a stake in the future. Find something to plan, dream and scheme about – a holiday, house move, new furniture, new look for yourself – anything that promises hope and delight.

Appendix 1

■ CANCER COMBINED WITH MOON SIGN

Our 'birth sign' or 'star sign' refers to the sign of the zodiac occupied by the Sun when we were born. This is also called our 'Sun sign' and this book is concerned with Cancer as a Sun sign. However, as we saw in the Introduction, a horoscope means much more than the position of the Sun alone. All the other planets have to be taken into consideration by an astrologer. Of great importance is the position of the Moon.

The Moon completes a tour of the zodiac in about twenty-eight days, changing sign every two days or so. The Moon relates to our instincts, responses, reactions, habits, comfort zone and 'where we live' emotionally – and sometimes physically. It is very important in respect of our intuitional abilities and our capacity to feel part of our environment, but because what the Moon rules is usually non-verbal and non-rational; it has been neglected. This has meant that our lives have become lop-sided. Learning to be friends with our instincts can lead to greater well-being and wholeness.

Consult the table on page 82 to find which sign the Moon was in, at the time of your birth. This, combined with your Sun sign is a valuable clue to deeper understanding.

Find your Moon number

Look up your month and day of birth. Then read across to find your personal Moon number. Now go to Chart 2, below.

January		February		March		April		May		June	
1,2	1	1,2	3	1,2	3	1,2	5	1,2	6	1,2	8
3,4	2	3,4	4	3,4	4	3,4	6	3,4	7	3,4	9
5,6	3	5,6	5	5,6	5	5,6	7	5,6	8	5,6,7	10
7,8	4	7,8	6	7,8	6	7,8	8	7,8	9	8,9	11
9,10	5	9,10,11	7	9,10	7	9,10,11	9	9,10	10	10,11,12	12
11,12	6	12,13	8	11,12	8	12,13	10	11,12,13	11	13,14	1
13,14	7	14,15	9	13,14	9	14,15,16	11	14,15,16	12	15,16,17	2
15,16,17	8	16,17,18	10	15,16,17	10	17,18	12	17,18	1	18,19	3
18,19	9	19,20	11	18,19	11	19,20,21	1	19,20	2	20,21	4
20,21	10	21,22,23	12	20,21,22	12	22,23	2	21,22,23	3	22,23	5
22,23,24	11	24,25	1	23,24,25	1	24,25	3	24,25	4	24,25	6
25,26	12	26,27,28	2	26,27	2	26,27,28	4	26,27	5	26,27	7
27,28,29	1	29	3	28,29	3	29,30	5	28,29	6	28,29,30	8
30,31	2			30,31	4			30,31	7		

July		August		September		October		November		December	
1,2	9	1	10	1,2	12	1,2	1	1,2,3	3	1,2	4
3,4	10	2,3	11	3,4	1	3,4	2	4,5	4	3,4	5
5,6,7	11	4,5,6	12	5,6,7	2	5,6	3	6,7	5	5,6	6
8,9	12	7,8	1	8,9	3	7,8,9	4	8,9	6	7,8,9	7
10,11,12	1	9,10	2	10,11	4	10,11	5	10,11	7	10,11	8
13,14	2	11,12,13	3	12,13	5	12,13	6	12,13	8	12,13	9
15,16	3	14,15	4	14,15	6	14,15	7	14,15	9	14,15	10
17,18	4	16,17	5	16,17	7	16,17	8	16,17,18	10	16,17	11
19,20	5	18,19	6	18,19	8	18,19	9	19,20	11	18,19,20	12
21,22,23	6	20,21	7	20,21,22	9	20,21	10	21,22,23	12	21,22	1
24,25	7	22,23	8	23,24	10	22,23,24	11	24,25	1	23,24,25	2
26,27	8	24,25	9	25,26,27	11	25,26	12	26,27,28	2	26,27	3
28,29	9	26,27,28	10	28,29	12	27,28,29	1	29,30	3	28,29	4
30,31	10	29,30	11	30	1	30,31	2			30,31	5
		31	12								

Find your Moon sign

Find your year of birth. Then read across to the column of your Moon number. Where they intersect shows your Moon sign.

Birth year					Moon number										
					1	2	3	4	5	6	7	8	9	10	11	12
1900	1919	1938	1957	1976												
1901	1920	1939	1958	1977												
1902	1921	1940	1959	1978												
1903	1922	1941	1960	1979												
1904	1923	1942	1961	1980												
1905	1924	1943	1962	1981												
1906	1925	1944	1963	1982												
1907	1926	1945	1964	1983												
1908	1927	1946	1965	1984												
1909	1928	1947	1966	1985												
1910	1929	1948	1967	1986												
1911	1930	1949	1968	1987												
1912	1931	1950	1969	1988												
1913	1932	1951	1970	1989												
1914	1933	1952	1971	1990												
1915	1934	1953	1972	1991												
1916	1935	1954	1973	1992												
1917	1936	1955	1974	1993												
1918	1937	1956	1975	1994												

Ari Tau Gem Can Leo Vir Lib Sco Sag Cap Aqu Pis

Cancer Sun / Cancer Moon

You are an extremely sensitive person, but you are also enterprising. Although your approach is probably fairly unobtrusive, you are capable of achieving much. At your best you can tune in to the needs of others and know instinctively how these may be gratified. In the process you are likely to chalk up achievement for yourself, possibly financially. Your nature is deeply caring and nurturing. It is vital for you to develop sensible habits of self-nurture that make you feel good, and do you good, rather than merely looking after others and hoping they will take care of you in return – they may not. Learn to recognise, treasure and protect the depths of your own feelings and needs, and avoid compensatory habits such as comfort eating, drinking or smoking.

Cancer Sun / Leo Moon

Your dilemma is that you yearn for the spotlight but often fear to take it. This may leave you waiting in the wings and eating your heart out. You are both proud and self-protective and you absolutely dread to look a fool or have the mickey taken. You must learn to cope with this, roll with the punches and 'feel the fear but do it anyway' if you are to achieve satisfaction. Develop a skill that will get you attention – this is vital to you and you can take centre stage gracefully when you feel assured. Learn to adapt – if people laugh at you then laugh yourself and act the clown. Ask yourself what is worse, a few knocks or life in a dark prison of your own making. You have loads of initiative, enthusiasm and dynamism. Put it into action, but also remember that you are precious and valuable and you don't need the applause of any crowd to prove it.

Cancer Sun / Virgo Moon

You need to be careful that you do not wind up being somebody's doormat. You have a natural inclination to look after people, get things organised, comfortable and running smoothly. However, if you realise you are being taken for granted you will feel hurt and offended – and there will be those who will take advantage of your skills. You are certainly a capable person – make this work for *you*. Be careful you don't allow yourself to become stressed out, for you may worry a great deal – and don't take on too much at once. You are a 'fixer'. Generally you are a most careful and circumspect person – no one has to tell you to 'look before you leap'. Your attention to detail, order and precision forms an excellent basis for your constructive and creative endeavours, and you are capable of accomplishing much. Be careful that you do not become so pre-occupied with nitty-gritties that your pursuit of the more meaningful plan gets sidelined.

Cancer Sun / Libra Moon

Well, when is everyone going to hear what you really want, feel or need? It's not that you can't assert yourself, and you have your share of dynamism, but you do tend to see both sides of any case and you may well reason yourself out of your real feelings – if you ever knew what they were in the first place. You may go for 'peace at any price' yet rarely feel at peace with yourself. You may succeed in attracting attention through your charm and social skills, but this will rarely be what you need. Sometimes you may even act contrary through frustration, but still to no true avail. You are a talented person with the skills of a diplomat and a strong sense of aesthetics and harmony. Be prepared to build a caring relationship with yourself, first and foremost. The rest will follow.

Cancer Sun / Scorpio Moon

You are a passionate and intense individual, but you are very cautious indeed about where and to whom you display this, because you wish to protect your vulnerability. One of the chief difficulties you are likely to encounter is that of letting go of anything or anyone, even when you know the time is ripe. You possess a degree of inner harmony, and in certain areas of life success will flow for you. In general, you are honest with yourself – you know how you feel and you have the guts to cope with it. Your knowledge of human nature is profound and your intuition is uncanny when it comes to people and their motives. You need to be careful that you are not too readily swayed by subjective considerations – remember there are two sides to everything, and guard against being uncompromising. Sometimes you can display a ruthless streak, very much out of keeping with your general attitude of understanding and compassion.

Cancer Sun / Sagittarius Moon

That restless streak and that habit you have of speaking your mind almost without intending to sometimes involves you in embarrassing episodes and apologies! You hate it when you've upset someone because it is your intention to care and console – and yet you find that bright-and-breezy attitude finds a chink. Although you need security you must also have the back door open. It is hard to say which is worse – being stifled or exposed, and you need to be able to move freely to locate your comfort zone. You are likely to have a philosophical streak and to possess a rich imagination – your wisdom regarding human nature is enhanced by a vivid inner life and many adventures, small and large. Travel – physical and intellectual – is a 'must' and it is probable that some religious/spiritual belief will become important to you.

Cancer Sun / Capricorn Moon

It is very likely that you hide your feelings beneath a very hard shell. Security – especially in terms of finance and employment, may be a preoccupation, and you may pour your energies into a profession, or into amassing money, rather than risk anything as 'iffy' as relationships. You set yourself very high standards and you are afraid to fail. Some might describe you as a 'control freak' but you keep your emotions in check because you know where unleashing them might get you. Nonetheless you have a surprising degree of intuition, often with regard to financial matters, property and real estate, and you are shrewd as to the motives of others. One day you will need to have the courage to be vulnerable, if you are to find true warmth. In addition, you may be addicted to striving without having asked yourself what for and whether the standards you follow are your own or someone else's. Take special note of your dreams, for clues.

Cancer Sun / Aquarius Moon

Probably you are a friend to many, and your wide circle may rely on a sympathetic ear and a cup of tea *in extremis* – and yet you rarely let anyone really close or ask for help yourself. You far prefer to theorise about humanity in general and other people's psychology (about which you may be extremely clever) rather than to settle to a little honest introspection, or to let someone analyse you. Inside all your caring lies a kernel of detachment, and you can be unpredictable and even a little eccentric at times. Your need for change is sometimes at variance with your need for security – too much closeness frightens you, and you may prefer to champion a cause rather than to commit yourself to another person. Remember that true freedom comes from having confronted one's inner demons. True security comes by the same route – you can have both. Trust your intuition – it's good.

Cancer Sun / Pisces Moon

You are so kind, gentle, compassionate and imaginative that you are almost awash! Your back garden may well be full of strays and your kitchen full of sob stories, spilt out into cups of tea – or something stronger! Generally you are reasonably at ease with yourself, and while you give a great deal to others you reserve a private something, deep inside, for what might be called 'the eternal'. Being a creature of moonlight and magic you are aware that there is much that cannot be expressed, and you are able to immerse yourself in dreams and poetry. Strongly empathic, you take on the colour of your surroundings and you should be very careful of the company you keep, so that emotional vampires do not suck you dry, manipulate, use or confuse you. Do not be afraid to express what you want openly. You may have a tendency to use manipulative methods yourself at times, or play the martyr. Give yourself the opportunity to bring your visions to life.

Cancer Sun / Aries Moon

You have a demanding nature, and while you require a lot from others you do not always give back in equal measure. You may need to be the centre of attention. However, you have a warm heart and will always try to respond positively to appeals from others. Not always clear where your feelings originate, they may erupt in bouts of cantankerousness. Your impulsiveness gets you into trouble and you have 'foot in mouth' disease, which makes you feel just awful sometimes! You are a champion of the underdog and will often fight more for the rights of others than yourself – for although you seek to be noticed this is rarely in connection with your true needs. You are often generous. Learn to assert yourself with more fore-thought. When you are kicking up dust, ask yourself what the stampede is really about and what you really want. Try to anchor yourself in the 'here and now'.

Cancer Sun / Taurus Moon

Possessions and stability really are a 'must' for you. You have an eye for the value of things and are shrewd with money, although you may overspend on luxuries. Love, for you, needs to be shown tangibly by care for the comfort and welfare of another and carefully chosen gifts. In return, you are able to care, practically, for others. Most Cancers are excellent cooks and gardeners, and with you this is a virtual certainty. You can be quite introspective and need to have time alone – often you enjoy being in your home. However, you are a practical person, highly creative, with a love for the beautiful. You need to be careful that you do not equate love and security too closely with material possessions. Also you find it very hard to let go. You may need to remind yourself that your well-being may be best served by moving on, at times, and your true needs may not be answered by self-indulgence.

Cancer Sun / Gemini Moon

You may be a real chatterbox but sometimes your tongue doesn't wait around long enough to find out what you really want to say, let alone feel. Often you immerse yourself in what is stimulating and distracting rather than concentrating on what is happening inside. You may worry quite a lot, and you can be very moody, although you can also be extremely lively, too. You are aware of emotional dimensions to life, but cannot always get to grips with them, so while you are probably a good friend to many, you may not be such a friend to yourself. Something inside tells you that your feelings don't count or can be reasoned away – they can't. Use your quick, analytical mind to sort out where you are coming from and concentrate on 'being' in your body. When you achieve true self-acceptance, then your mental excursions will become deeply satisfying in a way you had not imagined.

Appendix 2

ZODIACAL COMPATIBILITY

To assess fully the compatibility of two people the astrologer needs to have the entire chart of each individual, and while Sun-sign factors will be noticeable, there is a legion of other important points to be taken into account. Venus and Mercury are always very close to the Sun, and while these are often in the Sun sign itself, so intensifying its effect, they may also fall in one of the signs lying on either side of your Sun sign. So, as a 'Cancer' you may have Venus and/or Mercury in Gemini or Leo, and this will increase your empathy with these signs. In addition the Moon and all the other planets including the Ascendant and Midheaven need to be taken into account. So if you have always been drawn to Aquarius people, maybe you have Moon or Ascendant in Aquarius.

In order to give a vivid character sketch things have to be stated graphically. You should look for the dynamics at work rather than be too literal about interpretation – for instance, you may find you do not have much difficulty with Aquarius, but you may be aware that you are both coming from a very different 'place'. It is up to the two of you whether a relationship works for it can if you are both committed. Part of that is using the awareness you have to help, not necessarily as a reason for abandoning the relationship. There are always points of compatibility, and we are here to learn from each other.

On a scale of 1 (worst) to 4 (best), here is a table to assess instantly the superficial compatibility rating between Cancer and companions:

Cancer 3	Libra 3	Capricorn 3	Aries 1
Leo 2	Scorpio 4	Aquarius 1	Taurus 4
Virgo 2	Sagittarius 1	Pisces 4	Gemini 2

■ CANCER COMPATIBILITIES

Cancer with Cancer

You two have done quite well to get together at all, after all the dithering and self-protective devices. However, now it's all romance, roses and domestic bliss, until you both get in a mood at once and go silent on each other. Be careful of this, for as you know how to please each other, equally you know how to hurt and manipulate.

As lovers   This is a beautiful and cosy combination. Sex is probably wonderful, as you are both sensual, responsive and concerned for the feelings of the other. Ms Cancer is relieved that she has at last met a man that she can trust, and her whole being blossoms in the warmth of this. Mr Cancer slowly comes out of his shell as he begins to see that it is safe to show his emotions and his vulnerability. You will both want a lovely home and probably a large family – take care that the children do not become between you. If things should go badly wrong between you it will be very hard for either of you to make the break.

As friends   Naturally you will have much in common. You may enjoy gossips about the family, and the various creative projects. You may enjoy wining and dining together – and you might have fun verbally shredding neighbours and colleagues, in private.

As business partners   You are both creative, careful and good with money – and you both worry. An injection of pizzazz from elsewhere could help.

Cancer with Leo

You are both warm hearted and each of you needs a lot of attention, but in rather different ways. Cancer understands Leo's need for the limelight and indulges this, although Leo might feel at some point that he or she is being treated like a child – which is true! Leo appreciates Cancer's care and solicitude, but may come to treat Cancer like a doormat. Cancer may take this quietly – very, *very* quietly – until the Lion can't stand being ignored.

As lovers Lots of warmth – you are both passionate people. Cancer unfurls under Leo's demonstrative nature. Ms Cancer is charmed by this larger-than-life man, whose vulnerability she senses and Mr Cancer begins to show his feelings when he appreciates that this lady is prepared to show hers. Each of you is possessive, but Cancer may misunderstand sometimes when Leo grabs the spotlight, while Leo becomes insufferable if Cancer cramps her or his style. Each of you is stubborn. Cancer must learn to be very up-front about feelings, and Leo must learn just a little patience for this to work. Leo is not always prepared to respect the sensitivity of Cancer, but is usually generous – if a little patronising, if Leo realises he or she has transgressed. Both need to be needed, and both are deeply appreciative of love.

As friends Leo can light up the life of Cancer, while Cancer offers a space of safety for Leo, who is more vulnerable than she or he will admit. With Leonine flair and Cancerian excellent catering you could throw some wonderful parties.

As business partners A creative combination. Cancer has imagination and a 'feel' for what will work, while Leo has style and a conviction that all is possible. However, Leo can be one of the most extravagant signs of the zodiac, so Cancer had better hold the cheque book!

Cancer with Virgo

You two have much in common for you are both circumspect, both practical (although in very different ways) and you both worry (again, in different ways). Domestic life is likely to be fairly important to each of you, although Virgo may find Cancer a bit relaxed on the housework front. If things start to go wrong Virgo may avoid the issue by fussing and faffing while Cancer dissolves in angst – so making Virgo even more nervous. Virgo can hurt Cancer bitterly by thoughtless criticism, while Cancer can manipulate Virgo into a state of neurosis by witholding and denying.

As lovers You each take quite a while to warm up, but the practised and restrained sensuality of Virgo answers something in Cancer who thaws and responds, so you encourage each other more and more by mutual approval and delight. After initial careful weighing Ms Cancer decides this man has much to offer her and might be trusted with her heart, while Mr Cancer decides this coolly provocative lady has hidden depths. It is unlikely that your partnership will set the world alight but you won't fizzle out in a hurry either. Cancer may wish for more dynamism than Virgo can muster, while Virgo may find Cancer's emotional demands perplexing. However, Virgo can encourage Cancer to be a little more objective, while Cancer can coax some emotional warmth from Virgo.

As friends Yours is a sober partnership, but you may quietly carry on enjoying each other's company for years. You may share interests such as collecting items – for instance, antiques.

As business partners This works fairly well, but Cancer may get a little frustrated at Virgo's restraint. Both of you may panic when things go wrong. Things will develop slowly – it would be better to have someone with plenty of Fire in the chart on board with you.

Cancer with Libra

Because relationships are so important to Libra this is the best Air sign for the Crab. However, to Libra it is the mental rapport, the idea of the relationship that counts, and Libra may be puzzled and suffocated by Cancer's need for closeness. Cancer may be hurt by the fact Libra keeps analysing what is between them rather than snuggling up. However, Libra hates to be alone, and with Cancer it is fairly certain loneliness will not have to be suffered. Cancer can benefit from Libran detachment without the pain of separation.

As lovers Love between you is a beautiful and touching scenario with much gentleness and consideration. Sexual feelings will be quite strong. Neither of you is terribly decisive about first moves and you may dance around each other for a while before commitment. However, despite the hesitation each is a Cardinal sign, so something will happen, sooner or later. Ms Cancer responds to the good impression at which Mr Libra excels. His friendliness and skill at conversation impress her, and she senses that he might have similar values. Mr Cancer is charmed by this feminine lady, whose detachment piques him, but whose forthcoming nature draws him out. Libra hates unpleasantness and will do his or her best to coax Cancer out of moods. These two are likely to have a lovely, tasteful home.

As friends The aesthetically pleasing is treasured by both of you. If your tastes coincide you may enjoy outings to galleries, exhibitions and concerts and buy each other well-chosen gifts.

As business partners A good combination. Cancerian imagination and Libran style make for an appealing and individual approach. Cancer is rather more careful with the money and can smell out a dodgy deal, while Libra can be a great salesperson and tactician.

Cancer with Scorpio

The similarity between you can be a boon or a curse. You both have very passionate feelings, you both hang on like limpets to what you have decided belongs to you, and you both know just how to hurt! Attraction between you can be very strong indeed – neither of you goes for half measures. Sometimes the intensity is almost too much, but you can both take it. The emotional voltage could power the National Grid, but you aren't likely to be giving it away. Both of you may be very private about your feelings to outsiders – this goes too deep, and is too precious for words.

As lovers Sexually you are wonderful together – very passionate. This is an important area for both of you. Neither of you is that eager to open up at first, being very self-protective, but as time goes by the relationship grows deeper and deeper. You both take it very seriously. Ms Cancer senses that this man can answer her need for security and emotional closeness. Mr Cancer feels that it might just be safe to 'garner up his heart' with this sensual and profound lady. This is one of the best combinations of the zodiac. The drawbacks are that you will know how to wind each other up and there are sure to be some unholy storms. Each of you is past master at emotional manipulation. However, the making up is pure heaven.

As friends If you two have decided that you get on well then your friendship could be a lifelong affair. There will be much wordless understanding, and each of you will respond with intensity to the vicissitudes of the other. Do be careful that at no times you truly wound each other – each of you is capable of taking mortal offence.

As business partners Caution rules okay? You won't lose money, but if you are to make it you will have to find a pinch of gamesmanship.

Cancer with Sagittarius

This partnership wasn't made in Heaven but in a place that will freeze over before Cancer *ever* forgives the Archer for her or his unreliability. The compulsive Sagittarian urge for freedom is utterly at odds with security-minded Cancer, making this one of the more uncomfortable zodiacal duos. However, attraction is often fatally strong, at least initially.

As lovers   Cancer may thaw to the passion of Sagittarius, who is an ardent, if not always subtle lover. However, each of those notes Sagittarius leaves pinned to the fridge, saying 'Sorry love, had to go to London/Paris/Ullung-do, back Sat' is another nail in the coffin. Ms Cancer, when she is young, may fall for the devil-may-care adventurer, sure he will love her and stay home, while Mr Cancer may give in to the advances of Ms Sagittarius – as long as she's not so obvious she dents his ego. If things go wrong it will be sooner rather than later. Sagittarius cannot understand the Crab and so he may be superior and dismissive, while Cancer's empty arms ache and she or he begins to plan an escape, and one day the Archer strides home to an empty house. However, this relationship *can* work, but it needs lots of effort. Sagittarius can expand the Crab's horizons while Cancer can show Sagittarius that emotional warmth isn't just fireworks.

As friends   You may enjoy outings and holidays together, Sagittarius can stimulate Cancer's sense of fun and there may be some laughs. Also Sagittarius is a *bon viveur* and Cancer has no trouble living up to that!

As business partners   Again, if you both work hard, this could be a success. Cancerian caution and Sagittarian adventurousness complement each other.

Cancer with Capricorn

Here two of the most cautious signs of the zodiac have formed a duo. The ambitious and highly practical Goat has much to offer Cancer in terms of safety and commitment, both of which are essential to the Crab. Each values durability and they may remain together in a dead marriage rather than face the gory postmortem of domestic dismemberment, and the sharing out of the possessions each values so deeply. Capricorn is sometimes a shade restrained for Cancer, who expects and gives a little more spontaneity, once commitment has been achieved.

As lovers The sexual side is usually excellent, although the Goat does tend to put work first. This suits the Crab to a point, especially if Capricorn is paying the mortgage and it is understood that the work is for 'us'. At other times, Cancer will misinterpret Capricorn as 'cold' while the Goat will feel irritated by 'soppy sentiment'. Ms Cancer decides this man can be just the bastion against life's vicissitudes for which she longs, and Mr Cancer, while he may take time to unfold, is reassured by this lady's capability (which he may mistake for 'motherliness' although it is rather different). In time this pair can build a home that is virtually a castle, with rather a dynastic and conservative – with a small 'c' – attitude.

As friends There is much about each of you that complements the other, and several similarities. You may both enjoy things of worth and dignity, such as antiques. If moods do arise, Capricorn deals with them pragmatically. Each of you appreciates both quiet and activity.

As business partners Pretty good, both of you are 'doing' types. Cancer has imagination and Capricorn is a 'Mr or Ms Fixit'. A little over-cautious, maybe.

Cancer with Aquarius

Here we have one of those fatally attractive and endlessly fraught Water/Air mixes. What is initially fascinating can turn into a tale of bewilderment and frustration, unless you each try very hard to understand the other. The good thing is that you each have your own brand of imaginative thinking – use it in your relationship.

As lovers Sexual pleasure may be intense at first, but after a while Cancer finds Aquarian unpredictable, detached phases unbearable while Aquarius resents the Crab's clinginess, and tries endlessly to analyse the moods, to no avail. On the plus side, Aquarius, while valuing the theory of freedom, is reasonably reliable when it comes to commitment – after all, one must Do The Right Thing. However, this does little to reassure the Crab and the two may end up living in an emotional refrigerator. Ms Cancer may be fascinated by this man's impressive mind – or at least his whacky ideas, while Mr Cancer is mesmerised by this self-sufficient woman. Ms Aquarius might have to make her interest obvious, however, before anything happens. The gentleness and solicitude of the Crab and the friend-liness and interest in life that Aquarius possesses can make a precious complement. However, this relationship needs lots of work and self-awareness from each.

As friends Without a sexual spark you'll have little in common, unless there are other shared chart factors. Aquarius can open Cancer's mind and Cancer can show Aquarius what feelings really are, as opposed to what they should be. Value each other.

As business partners Not a bad mixture, although all the above-mentioned drawbacks are bound to surface to some extent. Take care of separate areas of the work. Respect each other, implement Aquarian ideas and let Cancer handle awkward clients.

Cancer with Pisces

Here we have heart-and-soulmates. It's all wine, roses and wordless empathy, cosy fireside snuggles, moonlit meanders and dreams. This is one of the best zodiacal matches, for each of you lives on emotions. Cancer appreciates Piscean subtlety and endless understanding while Pisces feels snug and cared for. No one knows better than Pisces how to coax a Crabby mood. However, there are aspects to Pisces that Cancer may have trouble with, and unreliability is one of them.

As lovers   Love is ethereal and sex is sublime. You are both very passionate, expecting and giving a great deal in relationships. Ms Cancer sees all that her heart could desire in this subtle and gentle man, who evokes all her motherly instincts, while Mr Cancer finds this woman knows exactly (certainly better than any other in the zodiac) how to coax him into feeling safe enough to make a move so decisive it's almost macho – without 'coming on' herself. This love boat could find choppy seas, however, when Pisces goes physically or mentally absent, or when Cancer badgers Pisces to be what Cancer calls 'sensible' – which Pisces may see as boring, conventional and cramping.

As friends   This works really well. Pisces is an excellent repository for Cancerian worries and gossip, usually finding just the right things to say, while Cancer soothes Pisces, when necessary. Both do tend to worry quite a lot, however, and may work each other up or create a siege scenario – 'It's you and me against the world'.

As business partners   Possibly OK. Both of you are creative. Cancer is usually sensible while Pisces has endless imagination. Don't waste time chattering or being negative. Cancer has the purse!

Cancer with Aries

Cancer likes the assertiveness of Aries, whom Cancer sees as the type of person who can provide material wants. This may be true, but Aries also supplies a lot of what the Crab *doesn't* want – aggravation, impetuousness and tactlessness. No one can send the Crab into a mood quicker than Aries, or get Cancer searching methodically through the negativity cupboard for a wet blanket to throw on those wild Arien flames. Oh heavens, not again! This is a zodiacal combination for endless disagreements and frustration, but they do seem to love each other – at least at first.

As lovers Sexual attraction is probably strong. The ardent Arien approach reassures the Crab, although it is a little on the raw side, and romance may run high. Ms Cancer likes this man's forthright approach because it means she knows where she stands, while Mr Cancer, although he may recede from the lady's advances, at least rests assured he has the green light when he's ready to play macho. However, no one is better than Aries at treading on the Crab's claws, and then Cancer retreats into the shell. Aries prods and probes, then stamps and shouts – it's tears before bedtime and definitely no sex. Aries does need to learn to count to ten, and Cancer needs to be a little more expansive for this relationship to achieve its initial promise.

As friends You'll either click or you won't – if you do it may be because you share some ideal, for instance conservation. This may be easier than a sexual partnership if Cancer can get used to Aries 'telling it like it is' and being unavailable sometimes.

As business partners You may frustrate each other eternally. Aries is always wanting to charge off with some scheme while Cancer hauls in the reins. Don't get so locked in conflict you achieve nothing.

Cancer with Taurus

If this match isn't quite made in Heaven it is certainly rooted here on Earth. You share much – both of you like material security, both of you relish permanence and value comfort. No one can make Cancer feel secure with quite the thoroughness of Taurus, and Cancer can make life so smooth that it's a miracle if the Bull ever gets out of those slippers or up from the table. However, Taurus can be a little unsubtle for Cancer and may cause bruises to the emotions – and the Bull might not even notice if Cancer goes quiet and moody! Nonetheless, this is a lovely combination.

As lovers   The two of you are very sensual, and sex is likely to be wonderfully satisfying. Cancer equates Taurean physicality with emotional intensity, and Taurus thrives on Cancerian responsive-ness. Ms Cancer sees that at last she has found the rock on which she can build her home, while Mr Cancer slowly comes to believe this lady is as down-to-earth as she seems and will respond to his sexual and emotional needs. Family is often very important for these two and they may feel their home is a bulwark against all of fortune's slings and arrows – which to some extent it is. Cancer may get frustrated at the Taurean meat-and-two-veg approach, and Taurus may dismiss Cancer as 'fanciful'. Generally, however, an excellent match.

As friends   You may share many interests, such as cooking and gardening, fine wines and dining out. Probably you feel secure with each other. Cancer may need to coax Taurus into going out.

As business partners   Cancer is always cautious and when teamed up with a partner who is more than a little that way, then things aren't very likely to take wing. However, each of you does have excellent money sense, Cancer has 'feel' and Taurus practicality.

Cancer with Gemini

This is one of the more difficult Water/Air partnerships, but that doesn't prevent it happening, time after time! Also, because the signs are next to each other, planets positioned in the other's sign is a likelihood, and this will help compatibility. Gemini stands on the bank, fatally drawn to the Cancerian depths, fearing the plunge and talking about it. Cancer wishes than Geminian light-heartedness and sparkle would come to the Crab as easily. Trouble inevitably sets in when Cancer clings and Gemini flies off again.

As lovers Scintillating at first. Gemini probably says all the right things which temporarily soothes Cancer, although the Crab can spot insincerity at a hundred paces. But it's not that Gemini is insincere – it's just that feelings are funny things and ideas are much easier. For Cancer the 'idea' of love is worth about as much as a bent coin. Nonetheless there is an undefinable 'something' in Cancer that keeps Gemini around, wondering – and the Crab has his or her own brand of lunar changeability. Ms Cancer is overwhelmed by Mr Gemini's wit and panache, while Mr Cancer is entranced by this vivacious lady, and may well allow himself to make a cautious move. Lots of work and understanding needed.

As friends Gemini can add lots of sparkle to the life of Cancer and keep the Crab laughing. Cancer is that port in a storm that Gemini rarely admits to needing, but uses all the same. Cancer can lend Gemini depth – these two have a lot to offer each other.

As business partners You may get on each other's nerves. Gemini can run Cancer ragged, and may find it much easier to sell ideas and commodities to clients than to persuade Cancer to buy his or her schemes. Keep trying – if you can put up with each other the world may see you as a success.

Appendix 3

TRADITIONAL ASSOCIATIONS AND TOTEM

Each sign of the zodiac is said to have an affinity with certain colours, plants, stones and other substances. Of course, we cannot be definite about this, for not only do sources vary regarding specific correspondences – we also have the rest of the astrological chart to bear in mind. Some people also believe that the whole concept of such associations is invalid. However, there certainly do seem to be some links between the character of each of the signs and the properties of certain substances. It is up to you to experiment and to see what works for you.

Anything that traditionally links with Cancer is liable to intensify Cancerian traits. So if you wish to feel especially dynamic and assertive, soft colours and the scent of lemon balm will probably not help! However, if you want to be your caring, Cancerian best it may help to surround yourself with the right stimuli, especially on a fraught day. Here are some suggestions:

- **Colours**   Greens and blues, soft pastels, ivory, white, grey, sea colours, silver.
- **Flowers**   Gardenia, jasmine, lilac, lotus, rose, violet.
- **Metal**   Silver.
- **Stones**   Beryl, moonstone, sapphire.

Aromatherapy

Aromatherapy uses the healing power of essential oils both to prevent ill health and to maintain good health. Specific oils can sometimes be used to treat specific ailments. Essential oils are concentrated and powerful substances, and should be treated with respect. Buy from a reputable source. *Do not use any oil in pregnancy* until you have checked that it is okay with a reputable source (see 'Further Reading'). *Do not ingest oils* – they act through the subtle medium of smell, and are absorbed in massage. *Do not place undiluted on the skin.* For massage: Dilute in a carrier oil such as sweet almond or grapeseed, two drops of oil to one teaspoon of carrier. Use in an oil burner, six to ten drops at a time, to fragrance your living area.

Essential oils

- **Eucalyptus**   This antiseptic and healing oil is quite descriptive of Cancer. It is excellent for coughs, bronchitis, catarrh, cystitis, fever and skin problems. It is also a stimulant to the nervous system.
- **Myrrh**   This has been used in ceremonies since antiquity and was especially used for embalming by the Egyptians. It has good antiseptic properties and reduces inflammation – its scent is rather funereal, so avoid it if you badly need a lift.
- **Lemon balm**   This is also called Melissa. An excellent oil for Cancer. It acts as a stimulant and a tonic for the cardiac system. It is helpful for counteracting depression and nervous anxiety.
- **Rose**   This beautiful oil is very expensive. It is good as a general tonic and fortifier, and for the nerves, circulation and skin. It helps eczema, wrinkles and blockage of the pores, and is also said to be effective for women whose sexual drive is low.
- **Sandalwood**   A tonic for the reproductive system, this oil also has soothing properties to those who suffer from anxiety. It

is good for the skin and relieves itching. It also acts as an expectorant for dry coughs and acts powerfully on the genito-urinary system, making it good for cystitis. Its exotic fragrance is heartening.

Naturally you are not restricted to oils ruled by your sign, for in many cases treatment by other oils will be beneficial, and you should consult a reputable source (see 'Further Reading') for advice if you have a particular problem. If a problem persists, consult your GP.

Your birth totem

According to the tradition of certain native North American tribes, each of the signs of the zodiac is known by a totem animal. The idea of the totem animal is useful, for animals are powerful, living symbols and they can do much to put us in touch with our potentials. Knowing your totem animal is different from knowing your sign, for your sign is used to define and describe you – as we have been doing in this book – whereas your totem shows you a path of potential learning and growth.

The totem for Cancer is the Woodpecker, and you also have an affinity with Frog and Mouse. You were born in the Long Days Time. There is a difficulty here, for the North American lore is based on the seasonal cycle. For those of you in the Southern Hemisphere, it is worth bearing in mind the totems of your opposite sign, Capricorn. These are Goose, Buffalo and possibly Turtle, though Turtle is of the Earth clan. Goose time is called Renewal Time.

Woodpecker is known for its rhythmic drumming on the trunks of trees, pecking away ceaselessly until the goal has been achieved. These birds cling tenaciously, making their nests with great care. Woodpeckers drum sometimes for the pure joy of the rhythm. The sound they make has been likened to the drum of the shaman – one who makes spirit flights to other dimensions and expands consciousness. The shaman uses the drumbeat like a 'horse' riding on the beat, which intensifies the trance experience. For Cancer Woodpecker is a valuable link with the natural world and an invitation to greater detachment – as suggested by the ability of the bird to fly. In addition Cancer can become somewhat blinkered, concentrating on concerns that are close to home – the idea of shamanic flight is expanding to consciousness and suggests a way Cancers may use their imagination. I am far from suggesting that all Cancers should embark on a shamanic path. However, they can certainly benefit from deep meditation, creative visualisation and the idea of flight.

Contacting your totem

You can use visualisation techniques to make contact with the energies of your birth totem. You will need to be very quiet, still and relaxed. Make sure you won't be disturbed. Have a picture of your totem before you, and perhaps burn one of the oils we have mentioned, in an oil burner, to intensify the atmosphere. When you are ready close your eyes and imagine that you are your totem animal – imagine how it feels, what it smells, sees, hears. What are its feelings, instincts and abilities? Keep this up for as long as you are comfortable, then come back to everyday awareness. Write down your experiences and eat or drink something to ground you. This can be a wonderfully refreshing and mind-clearing exercise, and you may find it inspiring. Naturally, if you feel you have other totem animals – creatures with which you feel an affinity – you are welcome to visualise these. Look out for your totems in the wild – there may be a message for you.

Further reading and resources

Astrology for Lovers, Liz Greene, Unwin, 1986. The title may be misleading, for this is a serious, yet entertaining and wickedly accurate account of the signs. A table is included to help you find your Rising Sign. This book is highly recommended.

Teach Yourself Astrology, Jeff Mayo and Christine Ramsdale, Hodder & Stoughton, 1996. A classic textbook for both beginner and practising astrologer, giving a fresh insight to birth charts through a unique system of personality interpretation.

Love Signs for Beginners, Kristyna Arcarti, Hodder & Stoughton, 1995. A practical introduction to the astrology of romantic relationships, explaining the different roles played by each of the planets and focussing particularly on the position of the Moon at the time of birth.

Star Signs for Beginners, Kristyna Arcarti, Hodder & Stoughton, 1993. An analysis of each of the star signs – a handy, quick reference.

The Moon and You for Beginners, Teresa Moorey, Hodder & Stoughton, 1996. Discover how the phase of the Moon when you were born affects your personality. This book looks at the nine lunar types – how they live, love, work and play, and provides simple tables to enable you to find out your birth phase and which type you are.

The New Compleat Astrologer, Derek and Julia Parker, Mitchell Beazley, 1984. This is a complete introduction to astrology with instructions

on chart calculation and planetary tables, as well as clear and interesting descriptions of planets and signs. Including history and
reviewing present-day astrology, this is an extensive work, in glossy,
hardback form, with colour illustrations.

The Knot of Time: Astrology and the Female Experience, Lindsay River
and Sally Gillespie. For personal growth, from a gently feminine
perspective, this book has much wisdom.

The Astrology of Self-discovery, Tracy Marks, CRCS Publications, 1985.
This book is especially useful for Moon signs.

The Astrologer's Handbook, Francis Sakoian and Louis Acker,
Penguin, 1984. This book explains chart calculation and takes the
reader through the meanings of signs and planets, with extensive
interpretations of planets in signs and houses. In addition, all the
major aspects between planets and angles are interpreted individu-
ally. A very useful work.

Aromatherapy for Pregnancy and Childbirth, Margaret Fawcett RGN,
RM, LLSA, Element, 1993.

The Aromatherapy Handbook, Daniel Ryman, C W Daniel, 1990.

Useful addresses

The Faculty of Astrological Studies
The claim of the Faculty to provide the 'finest and most comprehen-
sive astrological tuition in the world' is well founded.
Correspondence courses of a high calibre are offered, leading to the
internationally recognised diploma. Evening classes, seminars and
summer schools are taught, catering for the complete beginner to
the most experienced astrologer. A list of trained consultants can be
supplied on request, if you wish for a chart interpretation. For
further details telephone (UK code) 0171 700 3556 (24-hour answer-
ing service); or fax 0171 700 6479. Alternatively, you can write, with
SAE, to: Ref. T. Moorey, FAS., BM7470, London WC1N 3XX, UK.

Educational

California Institute of Integral Studies, 765 Ashbury St, San Francisco, CA 94117. Tel: (415) 753-6100

Kepler College of Astrological Arts and Sciences, 4518 University Way, NE, Suite 213, Seattle, WA 98105. Tel: (206) 633-4907

Robin Armstrong School of Astrology, Box 5265, Station 'A', Toronto, Ontario, M5W 1N5, Canada. Tel: (416) 923-7827

Vancouver Astrology School, Astraea Astrology, Suite 412, 2150 W Broadway, Vancouver, V6K 4L9, Canada. Tel: (604) 536-3880

The Southern Cross Academy of Astrology, PO Box 781147, Sandton, SA 2146 (South Africa) Tel: 11-468-1157; Fax: 11-468-1522

Periodicals

American Astrology Magazine, PO Box 140713, Staten Island, NY 10314-0713. e-mail: am.astrology@genie.gies,com

The Journal of the Seasons, PO Box 5266, Wellesley St, Auckland 1, New Zealand. Tel/fax: (0)9-410-8416

The Federation of Australian Astrologers Bulletin, PO Box 159, Stepney, SA 5069. Tel/fax: 8-331-3057

Aspects, PO Box 2968, Rivonia 2128, SA (South Africa) Tel: 11-864-1436

Realta, The Journal of the Irish Astrological Association, 4 Quay Street, Galway, Ireland. Available from IAA, 193, Lwr Rathmines Rd, Dublin 6, Ireland.

Astrological Association, 396 Caledonian Road, London, N1 1DN. Tel: (UK code) 0171 700 3746; Fax: 0171 700 6479. Bi-monthly journal issued.